Ravello

Vietri Sul Mare

Scala

Minori

Atranti

Amalfi

ITALIA

WILD ROSEMARY & LEMON CAKE

WILD ROSEMARY & LEMON CAKE

A COLLECTION OF ITALIAN RECIPES

KATIE & GIANCARLO CALDESI

hardie grant books

MELBOURNE · LONDON

INTRODUCTION

If you ask the Amalfitani – the inhabitants of the southern side of the Sorrentine Peninsula – to define the boundaries of the Amalfi Coast, most will tell you it stretches from Vietri sul Mare to Positano, in the region of Campania. However, some will disagree (as Italians do) and tell you it stretches from the more westerly Punta Campanella to the more easterly Salerno. Many visitors will also take in Sorrento and Capri when they visit this area, which further confuses the boundaries, so we have included recipes from these areas too. In fact, we gave up trying to establish the exact geographical location of the Amalfi Coast and instead threw ourselves into enjoying its virtues, feeling that a cookbook shouldn't try to be an atlas anyway.

I am thinking the reason you bought this book is because, like Giancarlo and me, you may have been to the Amalfi Coast and wish to re-create some of the delicious dishes you ate there, such as lemon risotto, gnocchi alla sorrentina, acqua pazza or a perfect pizza. If you haven't visited yet but aspire to, save those pennies, sell something you no longer need or blow your savings and go! You won't be disappointed; the views really are jaw-droppingly beautiful and you'll dine on wonderfully cooked local food and wine in the most amazing clifftop hotels and restaurants.

The sheer excitement of taking in the views is slightly marred only by the erratic local driving, which is hair-raising to say the least; it is a unique experience that makes the Amalfi Coast even more memorable. The near misses with the scooters, cars and buses were countless. I was shouting 'Giancarlo!' at almost every turn. 'Relax,' said Giancarlo. 'How can I relax?' I shouted back. 'A car is about to reverse into us!' Good grief, now I know why they drink so much limoncello – you really do need a stiff drink at the end of the day to get over the experience!

A LITTLE HISTORY
(AND WHY THE FOOD IS LIKE IT IS)

Known locally as la Costiera Amalfitana, this area is rich with stories and legends that talk of famous heroes, nymphs and sirens. Even the name Amalfi is linked to the nymph Melphe, the apple of Hercules' eye. Legend has it that when she died he built a city high up on the cliffs where he buried her.

Another theory is that the Romans who lived there in the 4th century named it Melfi. Over time, more Romans moved to the coast and so Amalfi grew in size until it became one of the four maritime republics, having the same importance and power as Genoa, Pisa and Venice. The Romans left a legacy of richly flavoured food such as **garum***, a sort of anchovy essence now known as* **colatura di alici***. They also enjoyed roast chicken and suckling pig with sweet and sour sauce made with saffron and marjoram.*

This trend of strongly flavoured food continued during the Middle Ages. The rich bought pepper, nutmeg, cloves and saffron to spice up their food and show off their wealth, with some spices costing their weight in gold. The poor used local aromatics such as mint, rosemary and wild fennel seed.

By the 6th century, Amalfi was trading salt, timber, gold, silk, slaves and grain in exchange for gold coins from Egypt and Syria. While the rest of Italy was still working on a barter system, Amalfi had its own currency. Through trade with the Arabs, citrus fruits, aubergines and durum wheat were introduced to the area.

The 9th to 17th centuries saw constant attacks from Saracen pirates along the coastline. When the Normans took over the land in 1073 they built a series of towers so that when they spotted a pirate attack they could warn their comrades in the neighbouring towers of impending danger by lighting a fire. A total of 30 towers were built and many of these are still in use today, housing hotels and restaurants such as the Torre Normanna (The Norman Tower).

In 1131, Amalfi was taken by King Roger II of Sicily, then four years later by the Pisans. Although it lost its power the Amalfi maritime code, which governed maritime trade in the Mediterranean from the 1000s to 1500s, remained in use until 1570. In 1343 a tsunami destroyed the lower part of the town and port and it never regained its previous power.

The Turks made constant attacks from 1543 to 1587. After the battle of Lepanto in 1571, Amalfi came under the control of the Viceroy of Naples, who was a Spaniard, and a Spanish influence can be seen in some of the dishes today, such as *Zucchine Scapece* (see page 190).

In Edwardian times, the Amalfi Coast became the destination of choice for British aristocrats. Later, actors such as Humphrey Bogart, Greta Garbo and Sophia Loren brought fame to the area and now it is a flourishing tourist destination.

In recent years UNESCO has included the Amalfi Coast in its World Heritage sites, so no matter who you are or how much money you have, it is impossible to build anything out of place on this beautiful coast.

DA MONTE O MARE?
FROM THE MOUNTAINS OR THE SEA?

The terroir of the coast has shaped the diet of its inhabitants over the centuries. With only a few kilometres between sea and mountain it is unsurprising that as you walk into any local restaurant you will be asked if you would like to eat from the mountains (meat) or the sea (fish). It is also unsurprising that you will find combinations from both the land and sea, such as bean and mussel soup, spaghetti with clams and calamari stuffed with locally grown vegetables.

Further influences on the food include the unusual combination of ancient monasteries and modern hotels. Over the years, monks have worked with food and drink, creating liqueurs and keeping alive centuries-old techniques such as preserving fish and making sfogliatelle. However, it was the chefs in the hotels and private houses post-1950s that were called upon for a lighter, more inventive touch to many of their dishes by their customers. It is this lighter touch that separates and defines the cooking on the Costiera from neighbouring Naples. Giovanni, the chef at local restaurant Il Giardiniello, told me that Neapoletan cuisine was meat-based and heavy, whereas the food from the coast was lighter, featuring more fish, lemons and herbs.

*Though the food may be lighter nowadays, even in the best Michelin-star restaurants the food is generally based on the old **cucina povera** or **cucina casareccia**, the home-style way of cooking from the days when money was scarce but produce from the land and the sea was plentiful. It has always been an extremely healthy way to eat, consisting of a diet based mainly on vegetables. **Acqua Pazza** (see page 155), a simple dish consisting of sea bass or sea bream cooked in tomatoes, is a typical example of the belief that the flavour and freshness of the fish should shine through and not be masked by too many flavours. One resident told me that when she goes to a restaurant she always asks if they put wine in their **acqua pazza**; if they do, she chooses not to eat there!*

*From working with chefs and local cooks we found **la cucina amalfitana** (the Amalfi cuisine) to be simple cooking, often referred to as **la cucina espressa**, meaning quick and easy dishes to prepare.*

LEMONS

These bright yellow globes of sweet, perfumed juice, with a thick white pith and flavourful zest, have become the symbol of the Amalfi Coast. Their proper name is **sfusato amalfitano** and they were originally grown in China over 4,000 years ago. Over the years merchants transported the lemons to Egypt via sea and land where Arab traders eventually brought them to the shores of the Sorrentine Peninsula.

Lemons are available as early as January but their flavour improves in the summer. Used in both sweet and savoury cooking, they are everywhere and you will even find the leaves used to wrap fish or smoked mozzarella.

Lemons are often sold with their leaves so that you can tell how recently they were plucked from the tree: wrinkly leaves mean the lemons were picked more than a week ago. Every part of the lemon is used. The bright zest is not usually waxed and is full of essential oils. If you have ever seen a barman twisting a length of zest and setting fire to it, that's the essential oil burning. The zest can be finely grated onto pasta or risotto; the thick pith is used for candying; the juice is squeezed over almost everything, from potato salad to lamb casserole and fish; and whole lemons make a delicious marmalade.

OLIVE OIL

A local chef, Giovanni, told me that the local oils are lighter and less fruity than other Italian versions, making them ideal for the delicate Amalfi cooking as they don't overpower the subtle taste of the fish, for example.

Have two types in the kitchen if you can: a standard extra-virgin olive oil for cooking and a single-estate extra-virgin olive oil for swirling into soup before serving, pouring over your **Insalata Caprese** (see page 18) or finishing lamb or fish on the grill.

A note on oven temperatures: It has been assumed throughout the book that a fan-forced oven is being used. Please adjust your temperatures to 20°C (36°F) higher if you are using a conventional oven.

ANTIPASTI

APPETIZERS

As I stood on the beach in Praiano I was blown away by the range of colours around me, turquoise sea swam into azure sky, dazzling pink bougainvillea flowers decorated the old white church and bright yellow lemons seemed to glow in the light.

Antipasti literally means 'before the meal'. On the Amalfi Coast antipasti are presented as little plates of locally produced salami and cured meats eaten with olives, toasted almonds, sun-dried tomatoes, **crocchè di patate** (potato croquettes) and marinated anchovies. Also popular is smoked cheese, such as scamorza or provola, pressed between large lemon leaves and grilled until soft. Italians never stray too far away from bread: either focaccia or slices of salted pizza bread drizzled with local olive oil are served alongside antipasti. Alternatively you might be served pizzette, mini pizzas that are first fried then finished under the grill with mozzarella and basil.

ALICI
ANCHOVIES

Cetara is an unspoilt fishing village and home to shoals of shiny silver anchovies. Known as **alici** or **acchuighe**, they are the reason for the town's wealth and heritage. While the anchovies are often eaten fresh, Cetara is famous for **colatura di alici** – the juice that is collected from the anchovies while they are stored and pressed in salt. It has become the delicacy of the town and is served in every restaurant over hot spaghetti or linguine, usually mixed with garlic, chilli, olive oil and parsley.

The anchovies for colatura can only be caught between 25th March and 22nd July, when the shoals are plentiful. Pasquale Ferrara, a local boat-builder who has a passion for making **colatura** in wooden barrels, learnt the technique from the old fishermen and believes the real thing to be far superior to the shop-bought variety. If fresh anchovies are hard to come by, replace them with other small oily fish, such as fresh sprats.

ALICI RIPIENE

STUFFED ANCHOVIES

Many Amalfitani restaurants, such as the beautiful garden restaurant appropriately named Il Giardiniello in the town of Minori, defy the Italian tradition by serving anchovies stuffed with cheese. Two marinated fillets are pressed each side of a slice of provola cheese then breadcrumbed and fried. Served as a hot antipasto they are mouthwateringly good.

ALICI FRITTE

FRIED ANCHOVIES

To prepare these little fish for frying, first cut off the head and then remove the backbone and belly with your fingers, pulling up from the tail (see picture on previous page). Trim off the dark flaps of skin on each side and rinse clean under cold running water. Drain on kitchen paper, season and dip in a coating of flour. Fry in batches in hot sunflower oil until crisp. Drain again on kitchen paper to absorb the oil and serve with slices of lemon and a further scattering of salt.

Clockwise, from top: Stuffed Anchovies; Marinated Anchovies; and, Fried Anchovies.

ALICI MARINATE

MARINATED ANCHOVIES

Serves 6

250 g (9 oz) fresh anchovies or sprats,
    cleaned and backboned
juice of 1 lemon

For the dressing
75 ml (2½ fl oz) extra-virgin olive oil
1 clove of garlic, finely chopped
1 tablespoon finely chopped parsley
good pinch of salt
½–1 red chilli, depending on strength,
    finely chopped
1 teaspoon dried oregano
juice of 1 lemon or 1 tablespoon white
    wine vinegar (optional – taste first!)

While sipping a glass of sparkling Falanghina at Ristorante San Pietro in Cetara we savoured anchovies marinated with garlic and chilli, followed by a spoonful of Lemon Marmalade (see page 232) to cleanse our palate, which worked a treat. Try to find the freshest fish you can to make this recipe; the older the fish, the more likely it is to fall apart after marinating, so give it less time in the lemon to begin with.

Start by making the marinade. Lay the fish in a deep, flat dish. Mix the lemon juice with 50 ml (2 fl oz) of cold water and pour over the fish to cover, adding a little more water if the fish is not quite covered. Refrigerate for 4–8 hours, or until the flesh becomes pale and opaque. Drain and pat dry with kitchen paper.

To make the dressing, mix all the ingredients together (excluding the lemon juice or vinegar). Arrange the fish onto a serving dish and pour the dressing over. Add more seasoning or chilli if needed, and only then dress with the extra lemon or vinegar, if you feel it needs an extra punch. See the picture of the finished dish on page 9.

PEPERONI
IN BARCHETTA
STUFFED PEPPERS

Serves 4 to 6

4 red peppers
100 g (3½ oz) soft country style
    white bread, crusts removed
150 g (5 oz) Anchovy Pesto
    (see page 93)
2 tablespoons extra-virgin olive oil

One of my favourite dishes is this way of preparing stuffed peppers. In Cetara they make a type of anchovy pesto. This, combined with breadcrumbs, is the way Rosa, my friend Francesco's mother prepares stuffed peppers to serve as a light supper. For an antipasto, cut the peppers lengthways into four to make a smaller portion size. This dish works equally well with basil pesto.

Preheat the oven to 200°C (400°F/Gas 6). Quarter the peppers lengthways into four and remove the white pith and seeds. Lay on a baking tray and bake for 15 minutes.

Meanwhile, put the bread in a food processor and blitz into chunky rather than sandy breadcrumbs. Transfer the breadcrumbs to a bowl and mix with the anchovy pesto.

Remove the peppers from the oven and spoon in the filling, patting it down with your fingers. Drizzle with olive oil. Return to the oven and bake for 10–15 minutes, or until the peppers are soft and tender. Serve either hot or at room temperature with other antipasti or a crisp green salad.

MELANZANE FARCITE
ALLA ENZA
ENZA'S AUBERGINES

Serves 6–8

For the aubergines
3 aubergines (eggplants)
fine sea salt
2 tablespoons extra-virgin olive oil

For the topping
250 g (9 oz) cherry or round
   tomatoes, diced
2 garlic cloves, finely chopped
1 teaspoon dried oregano
freshly ground black pepper
4 tablespoons extra-virgin olive oil
10 anchovy fillets
small handful of parsley, roughly
   chopped, to garnish

Enza Milano and her family live in Praiano. Her mother is a chef and her father runs the restaurant Il Pirata.

Preheat the oven to 200°C (400°F/Gas 6). Cut the aubergines lengthways into 1.5 cm (3 inch) thick slices (you should get about 10 slices) and then use a sharp knife to make shallow criss-crosses in the flesh. Lay the slices on a baking tray lined with baking parchment and scatter with salt. Brush the top with olive oil and bake in the oven for about 25 minutes, or until soft and browned.

Meanwhile, make the topping. Mix together the tomatoes, garlic, oregano, black pepper and olive oil. When the aubergines are done, remove from the oven and spoon the tomato mixture over, placing an anchovy over the top of each slice. Return to the oven for 15–20 minutes until the tomatoes have softened. Transfer to a serving dish and scatter with parsley. Eat immediately or allow to cool to room temperature. This dish will keep in the fridge for a day or two but never serve fridge-cold.

Wild fennel lines the roads, rubbing shoulders with silvery olive trees. The bright yellow fennel flowers will be collected by the locals and dried. The seeds will be kept and used for flavouring sausages, salami or making the liquer 'fionocchietto'.

Clockwise, from the top: Stuffed Peppers; Hot Potato Croquettes; Tomato, Mozzarella and Basil Salad; Enza's Aubergines.

INSALATA CAPRESE

TOMATO, MOZZARELLA &
BASIL SALAD

Serves 4

300 g (10½ oz) flavourful ripe
  tomatoes
2 × 125 g (4 oz) balls buffalo
mozzarella
20 fresh basil leaves
salt and freshly ground black pepper
½ teaspoon dried oregano
3 tablespoons best extra-virgin
  olive oil

Originating from the island of Capri, this salad should really only be made in the summer, when tomatoes are sweet and flavourful. My favourites to use are the large misshapen **cuore di bue** *or* **marmonde** *varieties. Failing that, heirloom tomatoes often look beautiful and have a fantastic flavour. Don't be tempted to cut back on the quality of the ingredients – it has to be buffalo mozzarella or a great cow's milk* **fior di latte***, ripe, juicy tomatoes, fresh basil and, if possible, you can use a wonderful single-estate olive oil.*

Cut the tomatoes into 1 cm (½ inch) thick slices or quarter them if small. Cut the mozzarella into 1 cm (½ inch) thick slices or tear into thick shreds. Alternate slices of tomato and mozzarella on a serving dish, with a basil leaf in between. Season, sprinkle with oregano and drizzle with the olive oil.

CROCCHÈ DI PATATE

HOT POTATO CROQUETTES FILLED WITH SMOKED CHEESE

Makes 22–25 croquettes

500 g (1 lb 2 oz) floury potatoes,
such as Maris Piper

150 g (5 oz) smoked cheese, such as
scamorza affumicata or smoked
Cheddar

50 g (2 oz) ham or cooked bacon,
finely diced

50 g (2 oz) Parmesan or Grana Padano,
finely grated

25 g (1 oz) pecorino cheese, finely
grated (or more Parmesan/Grana
Padano)

2 tablespoons finely chopped parsley

2 free-range eggs, separated

salt and freshly ground black pepper

sunflower oil, for deep-frying

150 g (5 oz) breadcrumbs

*Pasqualina is the 80-year-old mother of the two owners of Il Pirata in Praiano. Every day she makes around 200 **crocchè** in this busy seafront restaurant. These are frequently served as part of an antipasto or as a snack with drinks. Instead of the bland frozen varieties I remember as a child, these croquettes are packed with flavour from the smoked cheese filling. They are rather moreish, so go easy or the snack becomes the meal.*

Boil the potatoes whole in their skins in plenty of salted water. This preserves the flavour and prevents the potatoes from becoming watery. Meanwhile, cut the scamorza into 3 × 1 cm (1½ × ½ inch) rectangles (you will need about 25 pieces). Set aside.

To check if the potatoes are done, poke the largest with a skewer or sharp knife: they should be tender inside. When there is no resistance, remove from the heat and drain. Hold the potatoes with a tea towel and peel off the skins using a sharp knife. Mash, preferably using a potato ricer, as this keeps the mash light and fluffy. Now use a large spoon or your hands to mix in the ham or bacon, finely grated cheeses, parsley, egg yolks and season to taste.

Heat the oil so that it is ready for frying. Take a piece of mash the size of an egg and roll it into a ball. Put it into the palm of your hand and flatten. Place a rectangle of scamorza in the centre and fold the mash over to enclose it, making sure the cheese is completely covered. Repeat until all the mash is finished: you should have about 22–25 mini sausage-shaped croquettes.

Dip each *crocchè* into the egg white and then coat in the breadcrumbs. Fry in batches until golden brown and drain on kitchen paper. Serve immediately, while the cheese is still soft inside. See the finished Croquettes on page 17.

MOZZARELLA IN CARROZZA

DEEP-FRIED MOZZARELLA SANDWICHES

Makes 4

160 g (5½ oz) ball buffalo mozzarella,
    cut into 1 cm (½ inch) slices
8 slices soft white bread,
    crusts removed
3 eggs, beaten
8 anchovy fillets (optional)
handful of basil leaves (optional)
salt and freshly ground black pepper
300 ml (10 fl oz) sunflower oil,
    for deep frying
150 g (5 oz/2 cups) fine dry
    breadcrumbs, for coating
1 quantity of Quick Canned Cherry
    tomato sauce made with
    400 g/14 oz can tomatoes,
    see page 98), to serve (optional)

Originally made without anchovies or basil (but better with one or the other, in my opinion), this salty little fried sandwich is served as an appetizer. Many people prefer to use cow's milk mozzarella rather than buffalo mozzarella as it is less watery, but if you drain the cheese in a sieve or lay it briefly on kitchen paper the more flavourful buffalo mozzarella makes these little sandwiches even more delicious. The name of this recipe translates literally as 'mozzarella in a carriage'. Though no one seems to know where the name comes from, milk was once carried in wooden caskets and during its journey it would sometimes split and look like cheese. Serve as they come or with a tomato sauce.

Place the mozzarella slices in a sieve for at least 10 minutes to drain off some of the water. Lay 4 slices of bread on a work surface and brush the top of each slice with a little beaten egg. Lay mozzarella slices on top and, if using, half an anchovy in each quarter and the basil leaves. (If you are not using anchovy or basil, season with salt and freshly ground black pepper.) Lay a slice of bread over the top and press down to seal, eggy sides together. Put the sandwiches in a flat dish and cover with kitchen paper. Weight them down with a heavy plate or dish and leave for at least 30 minutes and up to 4 hours: this will help seal the slices together.

Heat the oil in a high-sided frying pan or deep-fat fryer. Dip into the beaten egg and coat with breadcrumbs. Fry until golden brown. Drain on kitchen paper for 2 minutes and serve with tomato sauce on the side, if using.

PARMIGIANA DI MELANZANE

BAKED AUBERGINE
LAYERED WITH TOMATO, BASIL & SMOKED MOZZARELLA

Serves 8

200–300 ml (7–10 fl oz) sunflower oil
   (add more if necessary)
4 aubergines (eggplants), cut into
   1 cm (½ inch) thick slices lengthways
2 × 125 g (4 oz) balls buffalo mozzarella
1 quantity of Winter Tomato Sauce
   (made with 2 × 400 g/14 oz cans
   tomatoes, see page 98)
25 g (1 oz) Parmesan, finely grated
25 g (1 oz) smoked provola or smoked
   Cheddar, finely grated
20 basil leaves for each mould, plus
   1 for each dome
crusty bread, to serve

The origin of Aubergine Parmigiana is argued about constantly by the regions of Sicily, Campania and Emilia-Romagna. It probably derived from Sicily, but don't tell the other regions! In this recipe, thin layers of aubergine (eggplant) are pressed together in a smooth tomato sauce. At Villa Cimbrone, a world-famous hotel in Ravello, it is served as individual domes with spots of bright green pesto around the tomato sauce. Pesto isn't essential but it does look pretty if presentation is key.

If you have time, salt the aubergines first to extract the water by sprinkling the slices with a little salt and draining them in a colander for 1 hour. It's a process well worth doing to prevent the finished dish becoming watery. If you don't have time to do this just use more kitchen paper to soak up the oil and juices after frying.

Heat the oil in a frying pan. Fry the aubergines in batches on both sides until golden. Remove from the pan and drain on layers of kitchen paper. (If you have time you can leave them in a colander to drain overnight without the paper.) Cut or tear the mozzarella into pieces and drain in a sieve for a couple of hours or overnight in the fridge.

Make the tomato sauce and purée with a hand-held blender or food processor until smooth. Preheat the oven to 180°C (350°F/Gas 4).

If using individual moulds
You'll need 8 semi-spherical moulds, 8 cm (3 inch) wide and 4 cm (1½ inch) deep. Line the moulds with aubergine slices, allowing the ends to flop over the sides as you will need to fold them over (there will be leftover slices that can be cut up and used for the layers inside the moulds). Add a spoonful of tomato sauce to each mould, then top with

layers of mozzarella, Parmesan, smoked cheese, basil leaves and aubergine cut to fit. Make sure you slightly overfill the moulds as they will sink during cooking. Finish by folding over the aubergine slices. Bake in the oven for 30–35 minutes, or until darkened and bubbling. Remove from the oven and allow to rest for 5–10 minutes.

Carefully invert the moulds onto a baking tray and leave for a few minutes while you heat up the remaining tomato sauce. Spoon a circle of sauce in the centre of each warmed plate. Using a fish slice, carefully place the domes on top of the sauce. Top with a little more tomato sauce and a basil leaf. Serve immediately with bread to mop up the sauce.

If using a lasagne dish

Pour one-third of the tomato sauce into a medium lasagne dish and lay over one-third of the aubergine slices. Top with one-third of the mozzarella, Parmesan, smoked cheese and basil leaves. Repeat twice more, finishing with a layer of tomato sauce (or the cheese will burn). Bake in the oven for 45–60 minutes.

Serves 4

8 courgette (zucchini) flowers
sunflower or olive oil, for frying

For the batter
100 g (3½ oz/1 cup) plain (all-purpose)
    flour
200 ml (7 fl oz) beer (or sparkling
    water if you prefer)
75–100 ml (2½–3½ fl oz/¼–⅓ cup)
    sparkling water
¼ teaspoon salt

For the stuffing
100 g (3½ oz) fresh ricotta
50 g (2 oz) smoked cheese, such as
    provola cheese or smoked
    Cheddar, grated
sea salt and freshly ground
    black pepper

To serve/garnish
Summer Tomato Sauce (see page 100)
    or ripe tomatoes, diced
few basil leaves, to garnish
basil oil, to drizzle

FIORI DI ZUCCA RIPIENI

STUFFED COURGETTE FLOWERS

For every courgette (zucchini) grown there are two flowers present on the plant: a male flower on the stalk and a female flower attached to the courgette. The male flowers have long, spiky stalks, which makes for easier dipping into the batter and hot oil, but when the courgettes are young they too can be fried along with the female flowers. Cut the courgettes almost in half, but not right through from the base to the tip to allow the heat of the oil to penetrate. I like to serve this dish with a little tomato sauce on the side. Otherwise, some diced fresh tomato is good, or a light salad of grated vegetables and a drizzle of bright green basil oil.

To prepare the flowers, pinch out the bitter stamens with your fingertips, trying not to break the flower and check for any bugs inside.

To make the batter, beat the flour with the beer (or sparkling water) in a bowl using a whisk or electric mixer to make a thick paste before diluting it with the sparkling water to the consistency of single cream. Add the salt. If any lumps remain, sieve the mixture before dipping in the flowers.

Heat the oil to 180°C (350°F) in a deep-fat fryer or high-sided frying pan, or until a small piece of bread dropped into the oil quickly turns golden and bubbles.

Meanwhile, mix the stuffing ingredients together in a bowl. Season to taste, but often the smoked cheese is salty enough.

Use a piping bag or teaspoon to fill the flowers with the stuffing, then twist the flowers at the top to close them.

Stir the batter (do this before each dip to keep the batter at the right consistency). Dip a couple of flowers into the batter and fry for about 3 minutes, until golden brown. Remove with tongs, drain on kitchen paper and keep warm. Continue dipping and frying in batches until you have finished. Serve with a dusting of sea salt and either a tomato sauce or a light tomato salad. Garnish with basil leaves and drizzle with basil oil.

CAPONATA

TOMATO, BREAD,
MOZZARELLA & BASIL SALAD

Serves 4

4 friselle or 12 Krisprolls
125 g (4 oz) ball buffalo mozzarella
   or *fior di latte*
4 small tomatoes or 8 cherry
   tomatoes, quartered or halved
15–20 basil leaves
1 teaspoon dried oregano
salt and freshly ground black pepper
3 tablespoons extra-virgin olive oil
1 tablespoon white or red
   wine vinegar

*This salad uses a local crisp brown bread known as **friselle** or **pane biscottato**, made from wholemeal flour and dried so that it lasts a long time. It is said that fishermen and sailors would take it with them, reviving it for lunch by dipping it into the sea. It is a great store cupboard ingredient even today, making a filling addition to a healthy salad. If you can't get hold of it, look for Swedish Krisprolls or similar instead. This recipe comes from Nicola Giannullo from Ristorante Rabbit, in Agerola. This **caponata** is not to be confused with Sicilian **caponata**, which is cooked and made with aubergines (eggplants).*

Soak the bread in a bowl of cold water for 10 seconds to soften it. Break into pieces onto a serving dish. Tear the mozzarella into bite-size pieces and scatter over the bread with the tomatoes, basil, oregano and seasoning to taste. Add the oil and vinegar and gently toss the salad with your hands.

VARIATION
To further enrich this salad add canned tuna, anchovies and boiled eggs.

MINESTRE
SOUPS

Soup takes many forms in Italy, from thin but flavourful broths sometimes enriched with an egg or pasta to hearty bean and pasta combinations that are more like stews. The chunky minestrone or fish soups thickened with bread are warm and filling. In poorer times, soups containing beans were a cheap but satisfying way of feeding the family during the cold winter months. Nowadays, soup is taken as a first course and either has pasta added to it or is eaten in place of pasta before the main course.

Following the coastal drive, I wound my window down to capture the breeze and another stunning vista at every turn.

ZUPPA DI PEPERONI ARROSTITI CON PATATE

ROASTED PEPPER & POTATO SOUP

Serves 4

3 red (bell) peppers
2 tablespoons extra-virgin olive oil
1 medium white onion, peeled and
    finely chopped
2 celery stalks, cut into 2 cm (3¼ inch)
    chunks
1 large garlic clove, lightly crushed
½–1 red chilli, depending on strength,
    finely chopped
1 large potato, peeled and cut into
    2 cm (¾ inch) cubes
salt and freshly ground black pepper
700 ml (24 fl oz/3 cups) homemade
    hot vegetable or chicken stock,
    or hot water
a large handful of spinach leaves,
    roughly chopped
good quality extra-virgin olive oil,
    to serve
Greek yoghurt (optional), to serve

This bright, colourful soup really caught my attention and now it is one of my favourite Italian soups – it just happens to be the colours of the Italian flag. It's always best to use homemade stock as stock cubes ruin the delicate flavour of this soup. If you haven't got time to make the stock, use water instead. Apart from the red peppers you can be very flex-ible with the ingredients: swap the celery for stems of chard and the spinach for either beet leaves or chard leaves to use up any seasonal vegetables.

Heat the oven to its maximum setting. Lay the peppers on a greased baking tray and bake for 20 to 30 minutes, or until blackened all over. Remove from the oven, put into a bowl and cover with clingfilm, or put into a plastic food bag to sweat. This will help to loosen the skins.

Meanwhile, heat the oil in a large saucepan. Fry the onion, celery and garlic over a medium heat until soft; this should take about 10–15 minutes. Add the chilli, potato and season-ing, and cook for a few more minutes, stirring frequently.

Peel the skins off the peppers and discard the seeds and cores. Save any water from the peppers as it can be added to the soup. Roughly chop the peppers and add to the pan. Stir through and add the stock or water. Cook until the potatoes are soft and just starting to break down, so that they thicken the soup a little. Stir through the spinach leaves until wilted. Serve in warmed bowls with a swirl of your best olive oil. (If the soup is spicy hot, cool it down with a spoonful of Greek yoghurt – not very Italian but delicious nonetheless!)

MINESTRA MARITATA
A MARRIAGE OF SOUPS

Serves 10–12

selection of pig parts, such as an ear,
 trotter, cheek or tail
6 Italian sausages
bone of cooked ham or proscuitto
2 carrots, roughly chopped
2 celery stalks, roughly chopped
1 large onion, halved
10 peppercorns
2 bay leaves
1 tomato
1 cabbage, such as savoy, shredded
60 g (2 oz) Parmesan rind
1 red chilli
salt and freshly ground pepper

This winter soup is not for the faint-hearted but the flavour is wonderful and it is well worth making, if only to use up often-forgotten parts of a pig. It is made from the trimmings left-over from salami- and ham-making, such as the bones, snout, trotters, ears and tail. Sometimes it also contains a chicken or a capon and sausages, as well as wild fennel. The soup is so called as it is a **maritata**, *or marriage of meat and vegetables, and is traditionally served at Christmas or Easter.*

If using a trotter, boil this separately from the other meat pieces. Boil the remaining meats, including the sausages and bone in 6 litres (12 US pints) of water, together with the carrots, celery, onion, peppercorns, bay leaves and tomato. Cover and cook on a low heat for about 3 hours, or until the meats are cooked through and almost falling apart. Put the cabbage, Parmesan rind, chilli, and seasoning to taste in a separate large saucepan and then ladle over enough stock from the meat pan through a sieve to cover the cabbage. Boil until the cabbage is tender: this should take about 15 minutes.

Meanwhile, discard the bones from the meat pot and cut up the meat and the trotter into bite-size pieces. Arrange in a large casserole dish. When the cabbage is cooked through pour it and the stock over the meat and serve. Reheat on the hob or in the oven if necessary until piping hot.

LA CASSUOLA O ZUPPA DI PESCE

SEAFOOD SOUP

Serves 4

1 kg (2 lb 3 oz) mixed fish and shellfish,
   such as clams, mussels, crayfish,
   squid, cuttlefish, gurnard and
   stone bass
1 shallot or ½ white onion
2 large garlic cloves
6 anchovy fillets
1 tablespoon capers, drained
handful of parsley
½ red chilli, depending on strength
6 tablespoons extra-virgin olive oil
salt and freshly ground black pepper
1 tablespoon tomato purée
100 g (3½ oz) canned or fresh roughly
   chopped tomatoes, depending on
   season and flavour
300 ml (10 fl oz/1¼ cups) hot water or
   hot fish stock
4 slices of white crusty bread,
   toasted

*The spectacular **cassuola** is named after the copper casserole pan it is usually served in. It is a mixture of what fish is available at the market, including langoustines, squid, mussels and clams. Often it is made with only crustaceans but it works just as well with fish too.*

First, pick over the shellfish, discarding any open or broken shells. Drop the clams into a bowl from a 15 cm (6 inch) height so that any that are open and dead or full of sand will split open and can be discarded. Clean any barnacles off the mussels and pull off the beards. Discard any that don't close. Cut any fish into 4 cm (1½ inch) cubes and the squid or cuttlefish into 1 cm (½ inch) rings or pieces. Set aside.

Using a large knife, finely chop the shallot or onion, 1 garlic clove, the anchovies, capers, parsley and chilli together. Heat the oil in a heavy-based casserole dish and fry the mixture slowly with a good pinch of salt and black pepper for 10 minutes. Add the tomato purée, then stir in the tomatoes. Season the squid and cuttlefish with salt and add to the pan. Pour in the hot water or fish stock and cook for about 15 minutes and add the fish. After 15 minutes, add the shellfish. Cook for a further 5–10 minutes until all the shells have opened, discarding any that haven't. Taste and adjust the seasoning if necessary.

Rub the toasted bread lightly with the remaining garlic and lay 1 slice in each serving bowl. Pour the soup over the top and serve immediately.

Serves 6

6 tablespoons extra-virgin olive oil

2 celery stalks, cut into 5 mm (¼ inch) pieces

1 red or white onion, cut into 5 mm (¼ inch) pieces

2 carrots, cut into 5 mm (¼ inch) dice

1 garlic clove, lightly crushed in its skin

1 palm-sized piece of prosciutto skin, or 2 slices of streaky un-smoked bacon, or 1 Italian sausage

1 bay leaf

salt and freshly ground black pepper

300 g (10½ oz) dried borlotti beans, soaked in water overnight, then drained

1 *mazzetto aromatico* (small bunch of herbs tied with string) of parsley, rosemary, marjoram and thyme

2 ripe tomatoes, skinned and quartered

1.2 litres (2 pints/5 cups) hot vegetable or chicken stock

1 teaspoon bicarbonate of soda

300 g (10½ oz) dried pasta, such as penne, some broken lengths or fresh pasta, such as maltagliati or cavatelli

For the spicy herb oil

3 tablespoons extra-virgin olive oil

a few sprigs of rosemary

a few stalks of marjoram

a few sprigs of thyme

1 tablespoon roughly chopped parsley

1 red chilli

2 garlic cloves, crushed

ZUPPA DI FAGIOLI

BORLOTTI BEAN & PASTA SOUP

*This was the most amazing dish I sampled on my travels in Amalfi! For such a so-called simple dish the family of cooks at Cumpa' Cosimo have really perfected this recipe, so much so that they wouldn't actually give it to me, so here is our equally delicious version made by Antonio Sanzone, the Head Chef at Caffè Caldesi. He told me that you should stir beans with a wooden spoon, not a metal one as it can affect the flavour of the beans. The herby **soffrito** and spicy herb oil are typical of the **contadina** or peasant style of cooking. While the soup rests off the heat, make the oil to finish it using seasonal herbs and then stir it in to give it the wow factor.*

Start by making the soup. Heat the oil in a large saucepan and gently fry the diced vegetables until soft with the garlic, prosciutto, bay leaf and seasoning. Add the drained borlotti beans and *mazzetto* and stir through. Add the hot stock and cook, covered, over a medium heat for 1–1½ hours, or until the beans are just soft. At this point add the bicarbonate of soda and cook for 10 minutes more.

Remove the soup from the heat and leave it to rest. Make the spicy herb oil by putting all the ingredients into a pan and cooking over a low heat until the smell of the herbs comes through. Stir the oil into the soup, remove the *mazzetto* and return the soup to the heat. Add the pasta, stir through and cook until the pasta is al dente. If the pasta absorbs too much liquid add a little hot water. Serve in warmed bowls.

ZUPPA CON FAGIOLI & COZZE

CANNELLINI BEAN & MUSSEL SOUP

**Serves 4 as a main course or
6 as a starter**

6 tablespoons extra-virgin olive oil
2 celery stalks, cut into 5 mm
    (¼ inch) dice
1 red or white onion, cut into 5 mm
    (¼ inch) dice
2 carrots, cut into 5 mm (¼ inch) dice
2 garlic cloves, lightly crushed
2 bay leaves
salt and freshly ground black pepper
300 g (10½ oz) dried cannellini beans,
    soaked in water overnight,
    then drained
1.5 litres (2⅔ pints/6⅓ cups) hot
    vegetable stock
½ teaspoon bicarbonate of soda
600 g (1lb 5 oz) mussels, cleaned and
    beards removed
1 red chilli, finely chopped
a few sprigs of flat-leaf parsley,
    roughly chopped
100 ml (3½ fl oz/½ cup) white wine

Heat half the oil in a large saucepan and fry the diced vegetables until soft with 1 garlic clove, the bay leaves, and a little salt and black pepper. Add the cannellini beans and stir through. Add the hot stock and cook, covered, over a medium heat for 1–1½ hours, or until the beans are just soft. Add the bicarbonate of soda, stir through and cook for a further 10 minutes. Remove from the heat. Now decide if you like the soup as it is or purée one-third of it to obtain a thicker consistency.

Heat the remaining oil in a frying pan over a medium to high heat. Add the mussels with the chilli, parsley and the remaining garlic. Shake the pan and pour in the white wine. Cover and cook for 8–10 minutes, until the shells have all opened. Remove from the heat and allow the mussels to cool slightly. Drain the mussels through a colander over the soup pan so that their juices are added to the soup. Remove most of the mussels from their shells but set aside a few in their shells for garnishing. Discard any mussels that have not opened. Stir the mussels into the soup and serve immediately, garnished with a few in their shells.

PANE &
PIZZA

BREAD & PIZZA

Eating simply cooked food in glorious sunshine while watching the crystal clear sea is my idea of heaven.

*Where there is a table of food in Italy, there is bread. No Italian ever eats a meal without bread. It is unthinkable to leave your pasta bowl or plate with sauce still clinging to it – much better to mop it all up with a hunk of bread. They even have a word for it – **la scarpetta** is the piece of bread used for such a purpose. In the Catholic religion bread represents the body of Christ and as such is treated with respect. I have seen people kissing bread before throwing it away or admonishing children for playing with it. Bread even has its own special day in the calendar: on 13th June it is the celebration of Sant'Antonio da Padova and it is traditional to bring bread to the local church to be blessed.*

Pizza al Metro

A FEW TIPS

YEAST

Fresh yeast, a by-product of the brewing industry, is a purer product than dried yeast as it has no additives or preservatives. It keeps for about three weeks in the fridge in an airtight container or can be frozen and used straight from the freezer. It keeps for up to three months when frozen.

Dried yeast is a more processed product with a much longer shelf life of around a year. It tends to come in sachets of 7 g (¼ oz) and can contain an active ingredient to speed up the rising of the dough. As a rule of thumb, you need twice as much fresh yeast to dried. Check the packet instructions – most active easy-blend dried yeast can be added straight to the flour, but some need to be mixed with water first like fresh yeast.

How much yeast should you use? Even a tiny amount of yeast will make dough rise. If you're making bread for the next day, use less yeast and rise the dough slowly in the fridge overnight, like pizza-makers do. If you need bread in a hurry, add more yeast to speed up the process but bear in mind that the slower the rise, the better the flavour, so if you want that wonderful slightly acidic aroma to your crust leave the dough to rise slowly.

FLOUR

Strong flours (from strong wheat, often American or Canadian) are ideal for making bread as they contain more gluten, which gives the dough its elasticity and helps the loaf keep its shape. They are perfect for making focaccia or a loaf but because of their nature the dough is hard to roll out and will shrink back, so they are not great for making pizza.

Type '00' flour is very fine, almost like talcum powder. It is made from soft wheat and doesn't have such elasticity or high gluten levels as strong flour, making it perfect for pizza, pasta, biscuits and sauces. Since being introduced to '00' flour I no longer use plain flour at all.

Wholemeal flour has had nothing stripped from it and is therefore more of a whole, unrefined product. Used on its own it would make a fairly heavy pizza base but, in the Pizza Al Metro recipe on page 62 it is mixed with some '00' flour to lighten it.

PIZZETTE
MINI PIZZAS

Makes 8 pizzette or 16 mini pizzette

250 g (9 oz/2 cups) '00' flour
50 g (2 oz/1/3 cup) strong white flour
15 g (1/2 oz) fresh yeast or 7 g (1/4 oz)
    of dried yeast
1 teaspoon salt
150–175 ml (5–6 fl oz/5/8–3/4 cups)
    tepid water
25 ml (1½ tablespoons) extra-virgin
    olive oil
sunflower oil, for deep-fat frying

Topping suggestions
Cherry or pizza tomato sauce,
    mozzarella and basil
Tomato sauce and smoked cheese,
    such as scamorza
Tomato sauce and salami
Pesto and mozzarella

These circles of light, puffy dough are fried and then finished in a hot oven or under the grill. They are usually served as antipasti on the Amalfi Coast. However, they are also great for a snack or light lunch with a side salad and can be made in advance (if doing this, fry the pizzette and top them only when you're ready to eat them). The even smaller mini pizzette are great for party canapés.

To make the dough, put the two types of flour into a large bowl and mix in the yeast and salt (if using fresh yeast blend it into a little of the water before adding it to the flour). Pour in the tepid water and olive oil and, using a dough scraper or your hand, blend the dough into a ball. If the mixture is very dry add a little more water; if it is very wet add a little more flour. The dough should be soft, light and pliable but should not stick to your hand. Tip the dough onto a floured surface and knead for 10 minutes.

Put the dough back in the bowl, cover with a tea towel and allow to rise. When it has doubled in size divide the dough into 8 even-sized balls and leave on a floured surface, covered with a slightly damp tea towel, to rise again for 30 minutes. Heat the oil in a deep-fat fryer to 180°C (350°F) or prepare to shallow fry. Preheat the oven to 200°C (400°F/ Gas 6). Now press or roll the dough into 11 cm (4½ inch) discs around 7 mm (1/4 inch) thick. Briefly fry until puffy and golden then drain on kitchen paper. Top with your favourite ingredients and finish by cooking in the oven for 5–8 minutes, until the cheese melts.

PIZZA

*Pizza dates back to Roman times at least, the word deriving from the latin word **pinsa**, meaning 'pounded' or **picea** meaning 'blackened'. It is thought originally to have been a piece of dough thrown into the oven to test the temperature of the oven. However, it soon developed into a popular street food, served dressed with olive oil and herbs – but it wasn't until Queen Margherita visited the Pizzeria Brandi in Naples in 1889 that a new pizza was created. The **pizzaiolo**, or pizza-maker, Rafaele Esposito fashioned a pizza in her honour in the form of the new Italian flag with red tomatoes, white mozzarella and green basil leaves. This really rooted pizza to Naples and it is still known as the place to find the best pizza in the world.*

*There are two types of pizza that reign on the Amalfi Coast: the long version sold by measure, **Pizza Al Metro** (see page 62) and the typical round pizzas expertly tossed in the air and topped with fresh ingredients. At the local restaurants the table bread will often be a pizza base covered with olive oil, coarse sea salt and fresh rosemary.*

PIZZA TOPPINGS

Pizza toppings tend to be the same from one restaurant to another but each establishment puts its own twist on a classic. Our favourites are:

MARINARA (TOMATO, FRESH BASIL, GARLIC AND OREGANO)

—

SALSICCE (SAUSAGE) AND TURNIP TOPS OR BROCCOLI

—

SMOKED SCAMORZA AND TOMATO

—

POTATO, GARLIC AND ROSEMARY

—

BITTER ESCAROLE MIXED WITH CAPERS, OLIVES AND PROVOLA CHEESE

—

ROASTED PEPPERS, OLIVES, CAPERS, ESCAROLE OR LETTUCE AND GARLIC

—

CAPRICCIOSA (MOZZARELLA, PROSCUITTO CRUDO, MUSHROOMS, ARTICHOKES)

—

CALZONE (MOZZARELLA, PROSCIUTTO CRUDO, RICOTTA CHEESE, EGG, PARMESAN OR GRANA PADANO)

PIZZA MARINARA

Makes 4

For the dough

500 g (1lb 2 oz/4 cups) '00' or plain (all-purpose) flour

2 heaped teaspoons salt

10–15 g (⅓–½ oz) fresh yeast or 7 g (¼ oz) dried yeast

300 ml (10 fl oz/1¼ cups) tepid water

2 tablespoons extra-virgin olive oil, plus extra to coat the dough balls

For the tomato sauce (makes enough for 4–6 pizzas)

400 g (14 oz) can Italian plum tomatoes

1 heaped teaspoon dried oregano

1 teaspoon salt

1 large garlic clove, finely chopped

2 tablespoons olive oil

a handful of basil, to garnish

This is one of the simplest pizza toppings, consisting of tomatoes, basil, garlic and oregano. Despite its name it does not contain any fish but instead was invented for the **marinari** *(sailors), who took bread and preserved tomatoes onto the boats. The high crust forms a harbour wall to the sea of tomato sauce. You can add various other toppings, such as mushrooms, mussels or whitebait, but never cheese or it ceases to be a* **marinara***.*

Start by making the dough. In a large bowl, mix the flour and ingredients together using your hands or a dough scraper. Blend the fresh yeast into a little of the water before adding it to the flour. Pour in the olive oil followed straight away by the tepid water. Mix the ingredients together using the scraper or the fingertips of one hand until you have a ball of dough. Depending on the strength and absorbency of the flour you may need to add a little more water to obtain a soft, pliable dough that is neither too sticky nor too hard. Do not be tempted to add more flour as a wetter, lighter dough makes a better base.

When you are happy with the consistency, tip the dough onto a floured surface and knead it by stretching, folding and turning it. The dough will snap and break at the start but after a few minutes it will have developed more elasticity. Knead the dough fast and rhythmically for about 10 minutes, until it bounces back to the touch – you should be slightly out of breath with the effort for 10 minutes.

Divide the dough into 4 even-sized pieces. To do this accurately, weigh the dough, divide the figure by 4 and then weigh each piece, adding or removing dough as necessary. Roll into balls. Gently wipe a thin layer of olive oil onto the surface of each ball and lay onto a floured deep-sided container such as a lasagne dish. Cover with clingfilm or a dampened tea towel and leave to prove until the dough balls are doubled in size. You can do this at room temperature or for a better flavour, put them in the fridge for at least 3 hours or overnight.

Meanwhile, make the tomato sauce. Put the tomatoes in a bowl and squash them with your hands or blend with a hand-blender. Add the oregano and salt, and stir well. The sauce does not need to cook as it will cook on the pizza.

Preheat the oven to its hottest temperature – a pizza oven is heated to about 400°C (752°F), so the nearer you can get to this temperature, the better. Turn 2 oven trays upside down and slide into the oven to pre-heat. This will mimic the hot stove of a pizza oven and will make it easier to shunt the pizzas onto them. After the dough has proved, use a rolling pin or your hands to stretch each dough ball into a 25 cm (10 inch) circle, or until the dough is about 5 mm (¼ inch) thick using plenty of flour to prevent it sticking. Transfer the base to a flat board or 'peel' (a flat wooden board) that has been lightly floured and top with the tomato sauce, leaving a border of at least 2 cm (¾ inch) all around. Scatter the chopped garlic over and splash with a little olive oil. Shunt the pizza quickly into the oven and close the door. The pizza should be ready after about 7–8 minutes – it is always best to slightly overcook rather than undercook your pizza to avoid a doughy base. Remove from the oven and leave for 2 minutes before slicing and eating.

CALZONI

FOLDED PIZZA CRESCENTS

Our favourite calzone is made by our friend from Ravello, Gianfranco Cioffi, who has now brought his skills to the UK and opened his own pizzeria and restaurant called Zero, in Ware, Hertfordshire. He divulged his secret to getting a 'nice and crispy' calzone: don't use tomato sauce, courgettes (zucchini) or any ingredient that holds water because it will make the dough soggy.

Preheat the oven to its hottest temperature. Roll a ball of pizza dough after it has risen (see page 58) into a 25 cm (10 inch) circle. Onto one half, pile on a couple of tablespoons of ricotta, some cow's milk mozzarella or drained buffalo mozzarella, a few slices of spicy salami, some fresh basil leaves, salt and black pepper. Fold the dough over to cover the filling and seal down the edges with your fingers or a fork. Bake in the oven until rich brown in colour and crispy. As soon as it comes out of the oven, spoon over a little tomato sauce for colour and flavour.

PIZZA AL METRO

PIZZA BY THE METRE

Makes 2 pizzas of roughly 28 × 35 cm, (11 × 14 inches) which fit on a standard-sized oven tray

For the dough

250 g (9 oz/2 cups) '00' flour
250 g (9 oz/1²⁄₃ cups) strong wholemeal flour
15 g (½ oz) fresh yeast or 7 g (¼ oz) dried yeast
3 teaspoons salt
330–350 ml (11½–12 oz/1⅓–1½ cups) tepid water

For the topping

ripe, flavourful tomatoes, or bottled tomatoes
4 slices of pancetta or streaky bacon
2 cloves of garlic, peeled and finely chopped
1 teaspoon dried oregano
salt
good quality extra-virgin olive oil, for drizzling
fior di latte (see page 249) or buffalo mozzarella

At the peculiarly named Ristorante Rabbit in Agerola (named after Jessica Rabbit in Who Framed Roger Rabbit) *where the famous fior di latte cheese is made, we watched Nicola Giannullo (this man's Pizza al Metro shots are on page 50) make pizza al metro using his favourite part-wholemeal flour dough. He told us the Agerola pizza is known as the 'day after pizza' as it is even better the next day. Nicola's tip is to add more yeast if in a hurry but he prefers to use just a few grams of fresh yeast for a whole kilogram of flour as he makes the dough at 8 am so that it has all day to ferment and rise before the evening service.*

Start by making the dough. In a large bowl, mix all the dry ingredients together using your hands or a dough scraper. If using fresh yeast blend it into a little of the water before adding it to the flour. Add the water and mix the ingredients together using the scraper or the fingertips of one hand until you have a ball of dough. Add a little more water if necessary.

Tip this onto a floured surface and knead for 5 minutes. Shape into a ball and put back into the bowl, cover with a tea towel and put it in the fridge to rise slowly (this usually takes about 7 hours) or leave it in a warm place to rise more quickly. The advantage of the slow rise is a better acidity to the flavour of the dough. Divide the dough into 2 even-sized pieces. Using your fingers squash and stretch the dough into two 28 × 35 cm (11 × 4 inch) rectangles or use a rolling pin if you prefer on a well floured surface.

If using a pizza oven

Transfer the dough to a long wooden paddle. Top with fresh or bottled roughly chopped tomatoes. Finish with pancetta or streaky bacon, garlic, oregano, salt, olive oil and fior di latte or buffalo mozzarella. Shunt the pizza in the oven and cook for 5–7 minutes. 'La pizza,' Nicola told me 'cooks in the front of the oven, away from the intense heat of the wood-burning fire.' This way the dough is cooked through but not burnt. See photo on page 50.

If using a domestic oven

Preheat the oven to its highest temperature. Put the pizza base on a lightly oiled baking tray then dress as above. Cook in the oven for about 10 minutes, or until the dough is cooked and the cheese is bubbling. It is always better to slightly overcook than undercook a pizza to ensure the base is cooked through.

VARIATION

Gigino Dell'Amura, the original owner of one of the biggest pizza restaurants in the world, invented the famous pizza al metro. His restaurant in Vico Equense is known as The University of Pizza and the speciality of the house is a metre-long (3¼ ft) pizza made on the long boards that are used to shunt the pizzas into incredibly hot ovens. They are made with a variety of toppings similar to *quattro stagioni*, or four seasons pizza, but with more choice. Each flavour is separated by lengths of rolled dough, which we thought looked great. We have been making them regularly since our visit with our children as everyone can choose their own toppings. My favourite is made with a tomato sauce base, then as soon as it comes out of the oven it is topped with a salad of lettuce or escarole if you can get it, olives, chilli, garlic, salt and olive oil. Giancarlo's favourite is a typically Tuscan combination of slices of cooked potato, rosemary, garlic, black pepper and sea salt. You can take a Tuscan to Amalfi but you can't take Tuscany out of the man!

Peach, apricot and lemon coloured houses crowd the base of the mountain in Positano facing out to sea and sunshine, encircling the calm waters of the bay below.

WHOLEMEAL
FOCACCIA

This wonderful focaccia can be made using the dough ingredients for the Pizza al metro recipe (see page 64). Preheat the oven to 220°C (430°F/Gas 7). Follow the instructions for the Pizza al metro recipe and after letting the dough rise the first time, shape it into an oval about 30 cm (12 inch) in length and 3 cm (1½ inch) thick and lay it on an oiled baking tray. Use your fingertips to make regular indentations and fill with fresh rosemary sprigs. Cover the surface completely with a thin layer of extra-virgin olive oil and allow the dough to rise and puff up to almost double the size: this usually takes about 45 minutes in a warm room.

Scatter sea salt flakes over the focaccia and bake for 17–20 minutes, or until it is golden in colour and firm to the touch. Drizzle over a little more olive oil and serve immediately.

RISOTTI & BRODI

RISOTTOS & STOCKS

Scooters weave in and out of dazzled tourists emerging from their coaches in the bright sun.

RISOTTO

Although risotto is more of a northern Italian dish originating from Lombardy and the Veneto, it is also made in the south, particularly in restaurants. The main rice used for risotto-making outside Italy is arborio, although it is the hardest to work with. It reaches its peak for just a few minutes when the risotto is perfect in texture but then continues to swell so that if you don't serve it quickly, you end up with a rather sticky result. Carnaroli rice is more forgiving in that respect and for a more watery sauce, such as one made with a shellfish stock, Vialone Nano is ideal.

STOCK

No self-respecting risotto would be seen without its perfect partner: homemade stock. When cooking a risotto make sure you have everything to hand before you start: ingredients chopped and ready, glass of wine, your favourite music playing, and so on. The more you reduce the stock, the more concentrated the flavour becomes, so you need less of it for a stew, soup or risotto. Freeze stock in a concentrated form, as it takes up less space.

BRODO DI VERDURA
VEGETABLE STOCK

6 tablespoons extra-virgin olive oil
1 medium white onion, cut in half
2 carrots, roughly chopped
3 celery stalks, roughly chopped
1 large tomato, with a small cross cut
   in the top
3 garlic cloves, crushed
6 long parsley stalks
a few sprigs of basil, with stalks
10 black peppercorns
3 bay leaves
3 litres (5¼ pints/12½ cups)
   cold water

Keep this light and delicate, and simply strain the broth from the vegetables or for a more robust flavour, purée the softened vegetables and add them too. I would recommend puréeing for a bean soup, for example, but keep the broth clear and light for the Lemon & Prawn Risotto recipe on page 74.

Heat the oil in a very large saucepan or stockpot and fry all the ingredients together. After about 10 minutes, pour in the water. For a light and delicate stock, bring to the boil and then remove from the heat, allow to cool and strain. For a more full-on flavour, cook for a further 30 minutes. Leave to cool slightly and strain, putting the vegetables into a *passatutto*, or food mill. If you do not have one, use a sieve instead and push the soft vegetables through with a ladle, adding them to the stock.

BRODO AI FRUTTI
DI MARE
SHELLFISH STOCK

5 tablespoons olive oil
300 g (10½ oz) lobster, crab or prawn
  (shrimp) heads and shells,
  or a mixture
1 white onion, cut into eighths
1 carrot, roughly chopped
1 celery stalk, roughly chopped (add
  the leaves and ends too if you like)
1 large tomato, quartered
handful of parsley stalks
3 litres (5¼ pints/12½ cups)
  cold water

It is well worth making this stock as the flavour is rich and impressive. It can always be frozen if you make a large enough batch.

Heat the oil in a large saucepan and fry all the ingredients together over a medium heat for 15–20 minutes, until they brown and start to stick to the bottom of the pan. Be brave and let them burn – this is our chef Gregorio's tip. Add the water and bring to the boil, then turn the heat down and simmer for about 40 minutes. Taste the stock and if the flavour is not rich enough simmer for a further 10 minutes.

For a subtle stock strain off the fish and vegetables and keep the liquor only. For a stronger flavour pick out any lobster or crab shells, leaving only the vegetables and prawn shells. Put all of this through a *passatutto*, or food mill, and grind. If you do not have one, use a sieve instead and push the soft vegetables through with a ladle. The stock will be thicker and much more flavourful.

RISOTTO AL LIMONE & GAMBERI

LEMON & PRAWN RISOTTO

**Serves 4 as a main course or
6 as a starter**

16 tiger or 8 jumbo raw prawns
   (shrimp), unpeeled and with heads
1.2 litres (2 pints/5 cups)
   light Vegetable Stock (see page 72)
2 tablespoons extra-virgin olive oil
50 g (2 oz/½ stick) butter
1 white onion, finely chopped
1 garlic clove, lightly crushed
salt and freshly ground black pepper
1 tablespoon chopped parsley
300 g (10¼ oz/1⅓ cups) carnaroli
   or Vialone Nano rice
100 ml (3½ fl oz/½ cup) white wine
finely grated zest and juice of 1 lemon
   (to taste)

*With fat juicy lemons growing all around the coast, of course the local chefs are going to use them in **risotti**. At Trattoria da Gemma in Amalfi this light and delicate lemon risotto is served with raw prawns (shrimp) that are split and laid on top of the rice to cook in the heat of the flattened risotto. The perfectly cooked grains of rice remained separate yet melted in my mouth. I have used a clear, light vegetable stock so that the taste of the lemon can shine through.*

Peel the shells off the prawns and remove the heads and tails. Reserve half the heads for the risotto and freeze the remaining heads along with the shells and tails for seafood stock. Split the prawns open by running the blade of a sharp knife along the back and remove the long black intestinal tract. If you can't see one don't worry – it means the tract is empty. Slice half the prawns into very thin, long slivers. Refrigerate these for later. Cut the remaining prawns into 3 and refrigerate.

Warm the stock on a low heat. Heat the oil and half the butter in a pan and soften the onion and garlic. Season and stir in the prawn heads and half the parsley. Cook until the heads turn pink and start to stick to the bottom of the pan.

Add the rice and stir through to coat the grains in oil. When the rice starts to sizzle, pour in the wine and stir constantly for about 4 minutes over a medium to high heat until it has reduced and then pour in a couple of ladlefuls of hot stock. Keep stirring and only add more stock when the rice has absorbed the liquor and you can see the bottom of the pan. Add the lemon juice (to taste) to the pan and just a pinch of lemon zest.

After 15 minutes stir in the chopped prawns (not the slivers). Continue stirring and adding more stock until the rice grains turn from white to translucent. Taste the risotto

and add more lemon zest and seasoning if necessary. Use a pair of tongs to pick out the prawn heads and garlic if you see it. Try the rice; it should be al dente. Remove from the heat, leaving the risotto a little on the watery side as it will continue to absorb the liquor. Do not worry if you have not used all the stock, and if you run out simply use hot water. Stir in the remaining butter and parsley and ladle into warmed bowls. Lay out the reserved thin slivers of prawns over the hot risotto and serve immediately.

RISOTTO
AI FRUTTI DI MARE
SEAFOOD RISOTTO

**Serves 4 as a main course or
6 as a starter**

1 kg (2 lb 3 oz) mixed seafood such
  as prawns, mussels, clams, squid
  (shrimp), or cuttlefish
1.2 litres (2 pints/5 cups) Shellfish
  Stock (see page 73)
2 tablespoons extra-virgin olive oil
25 g (1 oz/¼ stick) butter
1 white onion, finely chopped
1 garlic clove, lightly crushed
salt and freshly ground black pepper
1 tablespoon chopped parsley
300 g (10½ oz/1⅓ cups) Vialone
  Nano or carnaroli rice
100 ml (3½ fl oz/½ cup) white wine

*In the shady garden restaurant of Il Giardiniello in Minori,
Giancarlo and I tucked into this triumphant seafood risotto.
The flavour is all in the stock and the freshness of the
shellfish. Try to buy prawns that are uncooked and whole.
You can then make the stock from the heads and shells.*

Clean and prepare the shellfish and cut any squid and
cuttlefish into bite-size strips. Warm the stock on a low heat.
Heat the oil and half the butter in a pan and soften the
onion and garlic. Season and stir in the parsley and cuttlefish
(leave the shellfish until later).

Add the rice and stir through to coat the grains in oil.
When the rice starts to sizzle, pour in the wine and stir constantly for about 4 minutes over a medium to high heat until
it has reduced, then pour in a couple of ladlefuls of hot stock.
Keep stirring and add more stock only when the rice has
absorbed the liquor and you can see the bottom of the pan.

After 15 minutes, stir in the shellfish. Continue stirring and
adding more stock until the rice grains turn from white to
translucent. Taste the risotto and add more seasoning if
necessary; the rice should be al dente.

Remove from the heat, leaving the risotto a little on the
watery side as it will continue to absorb the liquor. Don't
worry if you haven't used all the stock, and if you run out
simply use hot water. Stir in the remaining butter and ladle
the risotto into warmed bowls.

RISOTTO CON PROVOLA
AFFUMICATA & PROSECCO

SMOKED CHEESE & PROSECCO RISOTTO

Serves 4 as a main course or 6 as a starter

1 litre (34 fl oz/4¼ cups) hot vegetable or chicken stock, or hot water
3 tablespoons extra-virgin olive oil
50 g (2 oz/½ stick) butter
1 shallot or small white onion, finely chopped
1 garlic clove, lightly crushed
salt and freshly ground black pepper
300 g (10½ oz/1⅓ cups) Vialone Nano or carnaroli rice
150 ml (5 fl oz/⅔ cup) Prosecco or sparkling white wine
100 g (3½ oz) smoked provola or smoked Cheddar

Smoked cheese is very popular on the Amafi Coast, and mixed with sparkling Prosecco it makes a rich and comforting risotto.

Warm the stock on a low heat. Heat the oil and half the butter in a pan and soften the onion and garlic. Season lightly as the cheese is quite salty. Add the rice and stir through to coat the grains in oil. When the rice starts to sizzle pour in the Prosecco (drink the rest of the bottle as you're cooking!). Stir constantly for about 4 minutes over a medium to high heat until it has reduced and then pour in a couple of ladlefuls of hot stock. Keep stirring and add more stock only when the rice has absorbed the liquor and you can see the bottom of the pan.

Add the cheese to the pan and continue stirring and adding more stock until the rice grains turn from white to translucent. Taste the risotto and add more seasoning if necessary; the rice should be al dente. Remove from the heat, leaving the risotto a little on the watery side as it will continue to absorb the liquor. Don't worry if you haven't used all the stock, and if you run out simply use hot water. Stir in the remaining butter and ladle into warmed bowls.

PASTA

There is a great history of pasta production in Campania. The famous **'ndunderi** *– a type of gnocchi made from flour and cheese – from Minori are from an ancient, possibly Roman recipe and have even been recognized by UNESCO as one of the first types pasta. The* **maccheronari,** *or pasta-makers, realized that Gragnano, further inland from the Amalfi Coast, had a particularly favourable, slightly humid climate which was perfect for slowly drying pasta. Today many Italians will only buy pasta from Gragnano as it is such good quality. Typical shapes include* **mista corta,** *a mixture of broken long pasta and short shapes perfect for soups.* **Paccheri,** *meaning 'slap', or* **mezzi paccheri,** *which are half the size, are large tubes often served with ragù or tomato sauces.*

HOW TO COOK GREAT PASTA

Always cook pasta in a large pan with lots of water so that it can move around freely and will not stick together. Salt the water well – add around one heaped tablespoon to a large pan two-thirds full of water. It sounds like a lot, but most of it will stay in the water. There is no need to add olive oil to the water.

It's really important to cook the pasta until just shy of al dente – still a little firm when bitten. When al dente, use tongs to lift long pasta such as spaghetti or linguine out of the pan and transfer directly into the pan containing the sauce so that a little of the cooking water mixes into the sauce to lengthen it. Drain short pasta through a colander and reserve a little cooking water for the sauce. The pasta will finish cooking in the sauce and absorb its flavour.

PASTA FRESCA
FRESH PASTA

Makes enough long pasta (such as tagliatelle) for 4 as a main course or 6 as a starter

200 g (7 oz/1½ cups) '00' flour, plus a little extra if necessary
2 medium free-range eggs, preferably corn-fed for colour
pinch of salt

The standard recipe for making fresh pasta is to use one egg for every 100 g (3½ oz/¾ cup) of '00' flour. In the south of Italy many add a little salt for flavour, some add water for elasticity or economy and some add olive oil to stop the pasta drying quickly. However, we mainly use only eggs and flour. We keep our own chickens, sometimes their eggs can be a little small, in which case a splash of water makes up the difference in size to obtain the perfect ratio.

Tip the flour into a bowl, make a well in the centre and crack the eggs into it. Using a table knife, gradually mix the eggs and flour, starting in the centre and working your way outwards. Keep mixing until you have a thick paste, then use the fingertips of one hand to incorporate the rest of the flour until a ball of dough forms. Remove the dough from the bowl and put it on a floured surface. Knead the dough by stretching and rolling it, adding a little more flour until it stops sticking to the palm of your hand, adding a little more flour if necessary. It should form a soft but firm ball that bounces back to the touch when prodded. It should be all one colour if well-blended, not yellow and white. If the dough becomes too dry, return it to the bowl and add a drop or two of water. Knead it again or use a food processor to blend together.

Wrap the dough in clingfilm and leave it to rest for 20 minutes or up to a day in the fridge. It is now ready to go through a pasta machine or to be rolled by hand.

VERY QUICK
PASTA SAUCES

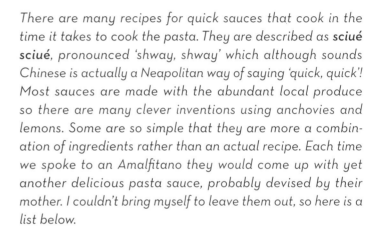

*There are many recipes for quick sauces that cook in the time it takes to cook the pasta. They are described as **sciué sciué**, pronounced 'shway, shway' which although sounds Chinese is actually a Neapolitan way of saying 'quick, quick'! Most sauces are made with the abundant local produce so there are many clever inventions using anchovies and lemons. Some are so simple that they are more a combination of ingredients rather than an actual recipe. Each time we spoke to an Amalfitano they would come up with yet another delicious pasta sauce, probably devised by their mother. I couldn't bring myself to leave them out, so here is a list below.*

After cooking dried pasta lengths such as spaghetti or linguine, drain and toss them into a hot frying pan with extra-virgin olive oil and one of the following combinations:

Salted anchovies, freshly ground black pepper and lemon juice

Lightly fried finely chopped garlic, parsley, chilli and lemon juice

Finely chopped toasted walnuts and chopped anchovies

Finely chopped fried red onion and salted anchovies

Although fish is not usually eaten with grated Parmesan, a scattering is often welcome.

QUICK PASTA SAUCES

TAGLIOLINI AL LIMONE

LEMON TAGLIOLINI

*I would like to share with you our restaurant chef Stefano Borella's tip for making dishes with a creamy sauce: use whipping cream. Double cream such as we have in the UK or heavy cream in the US is hard to get hold of in Italy. Italians use a thinner, lighter cream called **panna da cucina**, or cooking cream. The closest we have to this is whipping cream – it has the right fat content to blend with lemon juice without splitting and yet isn't too heavy to eat in a sauce.*

1 quantity of fresh tagliolini made with 2 eggs and 200 g (7 oz/1½ cups) '00' flour, or dried spaghetti or linguine

300 ml (10 fl oz/1¼ cups) whipping cream

juice of 1 lemon

salt and freshly ground black pepper

25 g (1 oz) Parmesan, finely grated

If using dried pasta, put this on to cook before making the sauce; if using fresh pasta make the sauce first. In a large frying pan, mix the cream, lemon juice, salt and black pepper checking for taste. Cook over a medium heat for about 5 minutes to reduce slightly and intensify the flavour. Tip the fresh pasta into the water now as it will only take a couple of minutes to cook. Drain the pasta and toss into the sauce with the Parmesan or Grana Padano. Make sure the pasta is well coated and serve immediately in warmed bowls.

FUSILLI CON GAMBERETTI, CANNELLINI & MENTA

FUSILLI WITH PRAWNS, WHITE BEANS & MINT

Serves 4

320 g (11½ oz) dried or fresh fusilli
 (page 122)
400 g (14 oz) cooked cannellini beans
 (either from a can or dried, soaked
 and cooked)
50 ml (2 fl oz/¼ cup) extra-virgin
 olive oil
½ red chilli, depending on strength,
 finely chopped
1 garlic clove, finely chopped
salt and freshly ground black pepper
16 raw tiger prawns (shrimp), shelled
 but with heads and tails on
100 ml (3½ fl oz/½ cup) white wine
12 mint leaves, roughly chopped
knob of butter

I ate this dish on our wedding anniversary at the beautiful San Pietro hotel just outside Positano. The waiter presented me with a ring from Giancarlo, my husband, hidden under a silver salver. Continuing a perfect evening, I then ate this delicate and exciting combination of fresh green mint and sweet pink prawns against a backdrop of pale cannellini beans and homemade fusilli.

Start by cooking the dried pasta in plenty of salted boiling water and make the sauce while it cooks. If you are using fresh pasta, make the sauce first and then cook the pasta.

Drain the beans and set aside. Heat the oil in a frying pan and lightly fry the chilli and garlic with a little seasoning, being careful not to let them burn. Add the prawns and fry until pink, then stir in the beans. When the beans start sticking to the bottom of the pan, pour in the wine and allow it to reduce for 3–4 minutes. During this time, cook the fresh pasta. Taste the sauce and season again if necessary. Scatter over the mint leaves over and stir in the butter.

Add the drained pasta along with a couple of tablespoons of cooking water and toss through the sauce. Serve in warmed bowls.

Tiny fishing boats go out and come in, the 'specials' in the surrounding restaurants reflecting the success of the fishermen's catch.

PESTO DI ALICI
ANCHOVY PESTO

Serves 8

60 g (2 oz) salted anchovies
    or anchovies in oil
50 g (2 oz) olives
50 g (2 oz) capers
30 g (1 oz) basil
1 large garlic clove
50 g (2 oz) parsley
50 g (2 oz) mixed nuts, such as
    almonds, hazelnuts, walnuts
    and pine nuts
300 ml (10 fl oz/1¼ cups) extra-virgin
    olive oil
1 small dry chilli
750 g (1lb 10 oz) spaghetti, to serve

Originally this pesto would have been made using a pestle and mortar but today a food processor is a quicker option. This recipe uses up the anchovies left over after making **colatura** *(below). We prefer salted anchovies in preference to those in oil; they should be well rinsed. If using the canned variety pour in the oil from the can too.*

Put all the pesto ingredients in a food processor and blend to a runny paste. I like to leave my pesto quite rough and crunchy, but blend until smooth if you prefer. Mix in with the hot spaghetti, along with a tablespoon of cooking water to lengthen the sauce.

COLATURA DI ALICI
ANCHOVY SAUCE

Though not readily available outside Amalfi, this unusual and delicious sauce deserves a mention. Otherwise known under its original Roman name of **garum**, *it is similar to the sauce made by the* **antichi romani**, *or Ancient Romans, who fermented various types of fish together to preserve them and strained off the resulting juices. Nowadays only anchovies are used, kept for 40 days in salt. The juice, or* **colatura**, *is strained and added to hot pasta with garlic, olive oil and lemon juice. This is the only time pasta is cooked without salt. The leftover anchovies are used for other dishes, such as Anchovy Pesto (above).*

PUTTANESCA
TART'S SPAGHETTI

Serves 4

3 tablespoons extra-virgin olive oil
1 large garlic clove, lightly crushed
½–1 fresh red chilli, finely chopped
2 heaped tablespoons black olives,
     pitted and halved
1 heaped tablespoon capers, drained
     and rinsed if salted
6 anchovy fillets
large handful of parsley, finely
     chopped
350 g (12 oz) cherry tomatoes,
quartered
salt, if necessary
350 g (12 oz) spaghetti, to serve

It is said that the ladies of the night would make this quick sauce for extra energy using their store-cupboard ingredients. However, our friend Michelina showed us this version made with fresh cherry tomatoes rather than the canned variety. I absolutely love the punchy, spicy flavours and cook it regularly for quick lunches.

Make sure you have all the ingredients to hand and then cook the pasta in a large pan of well-salted boiling water. Heat the oil in a large frying pan and fry the garlic and chilli, followed by the olives, capers and anchovies. Stir frequently to break up the anchovies. Add the parsley and stir through. After 2 minutes, add the tomatoes. Taste the sauce and season if necessary. Cook for another couple of minutes.

When the pasta is ready, use tongs to lift it from the saucepan directly into the frying pan, along with a tablespoon of cooking water to lengthen the sauce. Serve immediately.

VARIATION
Use canned tomatoes instead of fresh, and instead of the anchovies, gently stir through good-quality canned tuna at the last minute.

TOMATO SAUCES

It was the Spanish who introduced the golden rather than the red tomatoes to Italy in the 16th century. At first, however, it was only used as a decorative plant to be given as gifts as they were thought to be poisonous! Latini, the chef to the Spanish Viceroy of Naples, wrote his recipe for a tomato sauce called **alla spagnuola,** 'in the Spanish style'. However, tomato sauce with pasta appears for the first time in 1790 in the Italian cookbook **L'Apicio moderno,** by Roman chef Francesco Leonardi.

OUR FAVOURITE
TOMATO SAUCE

Serves 6–8

6 tablespoons extra-virgin olive oil
1 red or white onion, finely chopped
1 large garlic clove, lightly crushed
2 × 400 g (14 oz) cans whole Italian
    plum tomatoes
1 large sprig of basil
1–2 teaspoons caster sugar
1 level teaspoon salt
good pinch of freshly ground black
    pepper
12 ripe and flavourful cherry
    tomatoes, diced
550 g (1lb 3 oz) long or short pasta,
    to serve

This is our best tomato sauce recipe ever (in 17 years of writing Italian recipes!), using a combination of preserved and fresh tomatoes. Many Italians bottle their home-grown tomatoes in summer to eat throughout the cold months. Unless, like them, you have an abundance of tomatoes and the flavour has been ripened by the sun, this is the next best thing. The richness of flavour is much enhanced by adding half the oil at the beginning and half at the end, but you can cut down on the olive oil if you are watching your waistline. This sauce is perfect with both long or short pasta and is also good to use in the baked pasta dishes later in the chapter.

Heat half the oil in a frying pan and fry the onion and garlic slowly over a medium to low heat for 7–10 minutes, until soft. Add the canned tomatoes, then wash out the can with a few tablespoons of water and add this to the sauce. Add the basil, sugar, salt and black pepper, and continue to cook over a medium heat for about 15 minutes. Use a potato masher or fork to break up the tomatoes. Next add the cherry tomatoes. Cook the sauce for a further 15 minutes, then taste and adjust the salt and sugar if necessary. Stir in the remaining olive oil and your sauce is ready to mix in with your chosen pasta.

QUICK CANNED CHERRY TOMATO SAUCE

Serves 6–8

50 ml (2 fl oz/¼ cup) olive oil
2 garlic cloves, finely chopped
1 teaspoon salt
good pinch of freshly ground black
    pepper
2 × 400 g (14 oz) cans cherry tomatoes
1 large sprig of basil
2 teaspoons caster sugar
550 g (1lb 3 oz) long or short pasta,
    to serve

Canned cherry tomatoes are brilliant for making a simple sauce. Not only are they full of flavour, they're also peeled and as they're so small they cook really quickly.

Heat the oil in a frying pan and fry the garlic briefly with the salt and black pepper. When just soft add the tomatoes, basil and sugar. Break the tomatoes up a little with a wooden spoon and cook for 15–20 minutes over a medium heat. Taste and adjust the seasoning if necessary before mixing in with your pasta.

WINTER TOMATO SAUCE

Serves 6–8

6 tablespoons extra-virgin olive oil
1 red onion, finely chopped
1 garlic clove, lightly crushed
2 × 400 g (14 oz) cans whole Italian
    plum tomatoes
1 teaspoon sugar
1 teaspoon of salt
good pinch of freshly ground black
    pepper
550 g (1lb 3 oz) long or short pasta,
    to serve

This sauce contains no fresh tomatoes but relies on the knowledge of the Italian growers to pick and preserve their tomatoes when they are perfectly ripe. Always buy an Italian brand if you can and choose whole plum tomatoes over chopped as otherwise the cans contain too much juice.

Heat half the oil in a frying pan and gently fry the onion and garlic over a medium to low heat for 7–10 minutes, until softened. Add the tomatoes, sugar and seasoning, and cook over a medium heat for a further 30 minutes, using a potato masher or fork to break up the tomatoes. Taste and adjust the salt and sugar if necessary, before mixing in with your chosen pasta.

PACCHERI CON POMODORI FRESCHI

SUMMER TOMATO SAUCE WITH PACCHERI

Serves 4

350 g (12 oz) dried pasta, such as
    paccheri, penne, rigatoni or farfalle
4 tablespoons extra-virgin olive oil
1 large garlic clove, finely chopped
½–1 fresh red chilli, depending on
    strength, or ½ teaspoon dried
    chilli flakes
200 g (7 oz) fresh ripe tomatoes,
    roughly chopped
2 large sprigs of basil, leaves
    roughly torn
salt
25 g (1 oz) finely grated Parmesan
    or Grana Padano

Perfectly ripe cherry, baby plum or datterini tomatoes that burst with flavour are perfect for this dish. I love to use the heirloom varieties too for a dash of colour as well as flavour. Paccheri are large open tubes of pasta commonly used on the Amalfi Coast. They are great as they trap the cherry tomatoes inside. If you can't find them, try penne or farfalle instead. This recipe is from Michelina, the brilliant cook and owner of the beautiful Villa Maravilla in Praiano, where we shot many of the photographs for this book.

Make sure you have all the ingredients to hand and then cook the pasta in a large pan of well-salted boiling water. Heat the oil in a large frying pan and fry the garlic and chilli for 1–2 minutes, but no more as they will burn. Add the tomatoes, half the basil and some salt. Squash the tomatoes using the back of a spoon. When the pasta is just al dente, remove it with tongs and toss it into the tomato sauce, along with a tablespoon of cooking water to lengthen the sauce. Stir the pasta into the sauce and let it finish cooking – this way it will absorb more of the flavour of the sauce. Add the remaining basil and toss again. Serve in warmed bowls with a sprinkling of Parmesan or Grana Padano.

PASTA ALLO SCOGLIO

PASTA FROM THE ROCKS

Serves 4

350 g (12 oz) spaghetti or linguine
50 ml (2 fl oz/¼ cup) extra-virgin
    olive oil
2 medium squid, cleaned and cut into
    1 × 3 cm strips (½ × 1½ inch)
400 g (14 oz) fresh clams, cleaned
400 g (14 oz) fresh mussels, cleaned
4 raw king prawns (shrimp), with shells
1 garlic clove, finely chopped
½ fresh red chilli, depending on
    strength, finely sliced
handful of parsley, roughly chopped
50 ml (2 fl oz/¼ cup) white wine
12 cherry tomatoes, halved
good pinch of salt

Scoglio is Italian for rock, so this dish is made with crustaceans fished from the rocks and tossed into bouncy, al dente lengths of pasta. The salty seawater is released from the shells as they cook and flavours the sauce along with chilli, garlic and fresh parsley.

Bring a pan of well-salted water to the boil and cook the pasta until al dente. Heat the oil in a large frying pan, add the squid and cook through for just a few minutes. Add the remaining seafood, garlic, chilli and parsley. The shells will start to open in just a few minutes. When they are all open, pour in the wine and let it reduce for a couple of minutes. Discard any unopened shells. Then add the cherry tomatoes and salt. Drain the pasta and toss in the sauce. Serve on warmed plates.

PASTA CON BROCCOLI & SALSICCIA

PASTA WITH BROCCOLI & SAUSAGES

**Serves 4 as a main course or
6 as a starter**

3 tablespoons extra-virgin olive oil
1 onion, finely chopped
1 large garlic clove, finely chopped
salt and freshly ground black pepper
½ red chilli, finely chopped
250 g (9 oz) broccoli florets
400 g (14 oz) Italian sausages
75 ml (2 fl oz/⅓ cup) white wine
250 g (9 oz) orecchiette or short pasta
   such as penne
25 g (1 oz) Parmesan or Grana Padano,
   finely grated
best quality extra-virgin olive oil, for
   drizzling

Italian delis sell sausages that are perfect for this dish as they are made of pure pork and have no bread or rusk content. If you can't find them look for coarse-grained pork sausages that contain little or no wheat.

In winter porcini mushrooms are a good substitute for broccoli. Giancarlo stirs a couple of tablespoons of cream into the finished sauce to bind it together, though this isn't strictly necessary. This sauce is also eaten on its own without the pasta: in Praiano it is eaten in a sandwich and drunk with red wine for the feast of San Martino.

Bring a large pan of well-salted water to the boil and add the pasta. Heat the oil in a large non-stick frying pan and fry the onion over a medium heat for 5–7 minutes until softened. Add the garlic, black pepper and chilli and cook for a further couple of minutes, being careful not to burn the garlic. Only add salt later if necessary, as sausages are often salty. Meanwhile, steam or briefly boil the broccoli florets until just cooked.

Cut open the sausages and remove the meat. Crumble the sausage meat into the pan and break it up with a wooden spoon. Cook until browned, then pour in the wine and allow it to reduce for a few minutes. Keep the sauce over a low heat while you cook the pasta.

When the pasta is al dente, drain and add the broccoli. Add the pasta and broccoli to the frying pan, along with a tablespoon of cooking water to lengthen the sauce. Stir through gently, taste and adjust the seasoning if necessary. Serve in warmed bowls with a scattering of Parmesan or Grana Padano, a twist of black pepper and a drizzle of your best olive oil.

SPAGHETTI ALL'ARAGOSTA

LOBSTER SPAGHETTI

Serves 4

320 g (11½ oz) spaghetti or linguine
6 tablespoons extra-virgin olive oil
½–1 fresh red chilli, depending on
    strength, finely sliced
2 garlic cloves, lightly crushed
6 large raw prawns (shrimp), shelled
    but with heads on
1 cooked lobster, flesh removed and
    cut into bite-size pieces
salt and freshly ground black pepper
100 ml (3½ fl oz/½ cup) white wine
14 cherry tomatoes
handful of parsley, roughly chopped
crusty bread, to serve

As we watched the gentle waves roll into the beach at Praiano, during our research trip for the book, huge oval plates of this dish were being served at our local bar each day. The smell was fantastic. On some occasions there was no lobster because the fishermen hadn't caught any so it took us a few attempts to finally get to try this dish. Sometimes lobster can lack flavour, so we add a few prawns (shrimp).

Cook the spaghetti in a large pan of well-salted water. Meanwhile, heat half the oil in a large frying pan and briefly fry the chilli, garlic, prawns and lobster head and shell (not the flesh), and season. Add the white wine, cherry tomatoes and half the parsley. Cover and cook for a few minutes.

Drain the pasta just before it is al dente and add to the frying pan to finish cooking in the sauce so that it absorbs all the flavours. Add a few spoonfuls of the cooking water if the pasta looks a little dry. Add the lobster flesh to the pan with the remaining oil and parsley. Toss together – the pasta should look 'creamy'. Serve in warmed bowls with crusty bread to mop up the juices.

SLOW-COOKED PASTA SAUCES
& BAKED PASTA DISHES

These recipes take a little longer to prepare but are well worth the effort. Many can be frozen, so it's a good idea to make an extra-large batch for another day. A slow cooker is very useful for making sauces such as ragù or Genovese (see pages 112 and 120) as you can leave them to bubble away gently while you get on with other things. When making fresh pasta it's a good idea to enlist the help of friends or family. I was once told that making pasta isn't just about lunch; it's really about making time to catch up with others and giving yourself time to chat. I like that idea.

RAGÙ ALLA NAPOLETANA

NEAPOLITAN RAGÙ

Serves 8–10

200 ml (7 fl oz/scant 1 cup) extra-virgin
   olive oil
3 large carrots, finely chopped
1 large white onion, finely chopped
3 celery stalks, finely chopped
4 bay leaves
3 large garlic cloves, lightly crushed
6 Italian sausages
350 g (12 oz) pork ribs, cut into
   individual ribs
500 g (1 lb 2 oz) top rump or
   blade steak, cut into 4 cm
   (1½ inch) chunks
2 teaspoons salt
1 teaspoon freshly ground
   black pepper
200 ml (7 fl oz/scant 1 cup) red wine
2.5 kg (5½ lb) tomato passata or
   broken-up canned whole tomatoes
3 tablespoons tomato purée

All Neapolitan mammas have their own recipe for this intense, rich sauce. In fact it is more of a stew than a sauce as it contains roughly cut cubes or whole pieces of beef, often pork ribs and sometimes sausages. When the sauce is cooked, the tomato is spooned off from the meat and eaten with pasta for a first course, while the meat is served as a main course with vegetables. Old cookbooks dictate that ragù should be cooked for a whole day and many cooks still do this, which results in a glorious beefy tomato sauce. It is for this reason that the quantity of canned tomatoes is huge as they reduce during cooking. Many Amalfitani originate from Naples and have never had any reason to change the recipe. Ours is from our Neapolitan sous-chef Marco di Simone, who got it from his mother, who in turn got it from hers.

*A **soffritto** is a lightly fried mixture of vegetables, usually carrots, celery and onions, used as a base for ragù, stews and soups, providing a little sweetness to counteract the acidity of the tomatoes. The vegetables can be chopped by hand or very briefly whizzed in a food processor.*

Start by making the soffritto. Heat the oil in a large heavy-based saucepan. Fry the carrots, onion, celery, bay leaves and garlic over a medium heat for 15–20 minutes, or until soft.

Add the sausages, ribs and beef with the salt and black pepper. Brown the meat on all sides then add the wine and allow it to reduce for about 5 minutes, until the sauce is really dark and the wine has almost evaporated (I am often tempted to start eating it at this point as it smells so delicious!) Add the passata and the tomato purée and bring to the boil. As soon as the sauce starts bubbling, cover the pan and lower the heat. Cook on a low heat for 5 hours, or 8 hours if you can manage it, stirring every so often. Keep an eye on the sauce and add a little hot water if starts to look dry.

CANNELLONI

Serves 4-6

1 quantity of Fresh Pasta (see page 84)
1 quantity of Our Favourite or Winter
   Tomato Sauce (see page 98)

For the ragù
100 ml (3½ fl oz/½ cup) extra-virgin
   olive oil
1 large carrot, finely diced
2 celery stalks, finely diced
1 red onion, peeled and finely diced
1 garlic clove, lightly crushed
2 bay leaves
1 sprig of rosemary
300 g (10½ oz) coarse (not extra lean)
   minced beef
200 g (7 oz) Italian sausages, salami or
   prosciutto end
200 ml (7 fl oz/scant 1 cup) red wine
2 tablespoons tomato purée
salt and freshly ground black pepper
2 tablespoons ricotta

To serve
basil oil or olive oil for drizzling
   (optional)
shavings of Parmesan or Grana
   Padano
a few basil leaves, to garnish

The trick with cannelloni, as far as I am concerned, is to think about the dish you're going to serve it in and try to plan out how to cut and fill the pasta. Pasta swells by 30 per cent when cooked so you'll need to cut your pasta according to the size of the dish. I have given instructions for my lasagne dish but you could just as well cut the pasta sheets in half and make more small rolls. Cannelloni freezes well so I often double the recipe quantities and make two trays. The ragù uses strong-flavoured Italian sausages with no added rusk. If you can't find them, use diced salami or an end of leg of prosciutto (all of these are usually available from Italian delis).

First, make the ragù. Heat the oil in a pan and fry the vegetables with the garlic, bay leaves and rosemary for about 15 minutes, or until soft. Add the meats and brown them well. Allow any meat juices to evaporate before adding the wine and tomato purée. Cook the ragù for about 1 hour over a low heat, adding a little water if the sauce looks dry. Taste and add seasoning if necessary. Remove the pan from the heat and leave the sauce to cool. Transfer to a bowl, stir in the ricotta and refrigerate.

Meanwhile, make the pasta following the instructions on page 84. Roll the dough through a pasta machine so that its width spans the machine, which is usually about 14 cm (5½ inches). Put it through twice on the stop before last on the machine so that it is neither too thick nor too thin that it will fall apart. (The last setting makes the thinnest pasta but this is too fragile for cannelloni.) Cut the pasta into 11 cm (4¼ inch) lengths. You should end up with around 10-12 rectangles of pasta measuring 14 × 11 cm (5½ × 4¼ inches) and some offcuts.

Bring a large pan of well-salted water to the boil. Fill a large bowl with cold water and spread out 2 clean tea towels on your work surface. Cook the pasta for 2–3 minutes until al dente, then carefully remove the sheets with tongs and put into the cold water. As soon as they are cool enough to handle, lay them out on the tea towels to drain.

Preheat the oven to 180°C (350°F/Gas 4). Pour one-third of the tomato sauce into a lasagne dish measuring about 20 × 35 cm (8 × 14 inches). To make up the cannelloni, put 3 tablespoons of the ragù along one long edge of a sheet of pasta. Roll it up like a cigar and lay it in the lasagne dish. Repeat with the remaining sheets until the ragù is used up. (Any leftover pasta sheets can be oiled then frozen flat in a stack and used another day.) Pour over enough of the remaining tomato sauce to cover the cannelloni and drizzle over a little basil oil or olive oil, if liked. (Again, any leftover tomato sauce can be kept for a pasta sauce or frozen for another day.)

Bake for 25 minutes or until bubbling hot throughout. Either sprinkle the shaved Parmesan or Grana Padano over halfway through cooking time or when serving. Serve with basil leaves to garnish.

RAVIOLI AL LIMONE
CON BURRO & MENTA

LEMON RAVIOLI
IN BUTTER & MINT SAUCE

**Serves 4 as a main course or
6 as a starter
Makes 25–30 ravioli**

1 quantity of Fresh Pasta (see page 84)
semolina or plain flour, for dusting

For the filling
250 g (9 oz) ricotta
finely grated zest of ½–1 lemon
salt and freshly ground black pepper
½ teaspoon freshly grated nutmeg

For the sauce
125 g (4 oz/1 stick) butter
1 tablespoon roughly chopped mint
  leaves

Start by making the filling. Drain the ricotta then combine all the ingredients in a bowl. Go easy on the lemon zest as it can be quite overpowering, but as you want the flavour to shine through the pasta and sauce, slightly over-season rather than under-season. Bring a large pan of well-salted two-thirds full water to the boil.

To make the ravioli, divide the pasta in half and wrap one half in clingfilm. Flour the work surface, but do not flour the top side of the pasta or it will be hard to seal. Roll out half the pasta using a rolling pin or a pasta machine until you can see your hand through it. Set the machine to the setting before last – the last setting makes the thinnest pasta but this is too fragile for ravioli.

Cut the pasta into rectangles roughly the length of a cook's knife. Dot a heaped teaspoon of the filling at even intervals (two fingers' width apart is ideal) onto a length of pasta. Cover with another length of pasta and press down around the filling to expel the air and seal the pasta sheets together. Using a pasta wheel or a sharp knife, cut the ravioli into even 5 cm (2 inch) squares. Set the shapes aside on a surface dusted with flour or semolina (semolina is good as it does not stick to the pasta).

Cook the pasta for 4–6 minutes, until al dente – test by sampling the edge of a raviolo. Meanwhile, make the sauce by melting the butter in a large frying pan. When the ravioli are done, drain and add to the butter in the pan with a little of the cooking water. Shake the pan to amalgamate the water and butter and add the chopped mint. Serve immediately in warmed bowls or plates.

PACCHERI ALLA GENOVESE

PASTA TUBES
WITH SWEET ONION & BEEF SAUCE

For the sauce

2 kg (4½ lb) red onions, peeled and
    finely sliced into half rings
750 g (1lb 1oz) stewing steak
    (chuck steak)
200 ml (7 fl oz/scant 1 cup) extra-virgin
    olive oil
200 g (7 oz) carrots, coarsely grated
salt and freshly ground black pepper
200 ml (7 fl oz/scant 1 cup) water
175 ml (6 fl oz/¾ cup)milk
250 ml (8½ fl oz/1 cup) white wine

To serve

1 white onion, sliced into rings
flour, for coating
sunflower oil, for frying

The savoury but sweet combination of slow-cooked onions and beef is heavenly. This sauce is cooked for a whole day to achieve a deep, rich flavour. It can be made using tuna instead of beef, in which case the cooking time is reduced to 3 hours. The Genovese sauce is always served with paccheri – large tubes – of pasta.

Start by making the sauce. Put all the ingredients excluding the milk and wine into a large saucepan. Bring to the boil and then turn down the heat. Cover and simmer for 7–8 hours. After 1½ hours of cooking time stir in the milk. After another 1½ hours, stir in the wine. Check every now and again to see if the sauce looks dry; if it does, add a little more water. At the end of the cooking time, taste the sauce – it should be soft and sweet. Serve with onion rings dipped in flour and deep-fried until crisp.

FUSILLI FATTI IN CASA

HOMEMADE PASTA SPIRALS

Serves 4

300 g (10½ oz) fine semolina flour
3 egg yolks
50 ml (2 fl oz/¼ cup) water
1 teaspoon salt

*Fusilli were supposedly created in 1550 by the chef to the Grand Duke of Tuscany. Legend says that when he was kneading the pasta he dropped a piece on the floor. To amuse himself, his son picked it up and rolled it around a knitting needle. His father was so impressed by the shape he cooked it! When times were hard the eggs were left out of this recipe but including them does improve the taste, even if it makes you a little poorer! Originally these shapes were made around a knitting needle called a **fuso**, but any long, thin shape will do, such as a skewer. This type of pasta is often made with **semola rimacinata di grano duro**, which is fine durum wheat semolina.*

Pour the semolina flour into a bowl. Make a well in the centre and pour in the egg yolks and water. Use a knife to swirl the eggs and water together, incorporating the flour as you go. Gradually work this in, adding a little more water if necessary until you get a firm ball of dough. Wrap the dough in clingfilm and allow it to rest in the fridge for 30 minutes.

After this time pinch off a walnut-size piece of dough, keeping the rest covered. Over a wooden chopping board, use your palms to roll it into a length that is 5 mm (¼ inch) wide.

Dust a knitting needle with flour and wind this length around it in a long spiral, then roll onto the wooden board to flatten it slightly. Gently slide it off and set aside. Repeat until you have finished the dough. The lengths can be left long, like spaghetti, or cut shorter as you wish.

Alternatively, use a pasta machine to produce 20 cm (8 inch) lengths of tagliatelle on the setting before last on the rollers. Toss them in flour. Pierce the end of a length of tagliatelle with the tip of a wooden skewer to hold it in place and gently wind it around the length of the skewer. Do not roll it flat as above, as tagliatelle are already flat, but gently

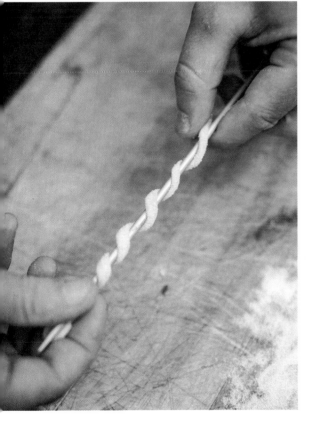

ease it off the skewer and set aside on a surface dusted with flour. Cut into 3 short lengths or leave as they are.

Bring a large pan of well-salted water to the boil. Drop in the fusilli. They will need 4-7 minutes' cooking time, depending on their thickness, until they are al dente. Toss into your favourite sauce and enjoy the fruits of your labour.

CRESPELLE RAVELLESI

RAVELLO-STYLE STUFFED PANCAKES

Serves 12 (makes two 20 × 35 cm (8 × 14 inch) lasagne dishes)

For the filling

2 tablespoons extra-virgin olive oil
1 white onion, finely chopped
salt and freshly ground black pepper
400 g (14 oz) good-quality sausages
75 ml (2½ fl oz/⅓ cup) white wine
400 g (14 oz) ricotta
100 g (3½ oz) cooked ham
75 g (2½ oz) Parmesan or
    Grana Padano, finely grated
200 g (7 oz) mozzarella or smoked
    scamorza, chopped into 1 cm
    (½ inch) cubes
2 large eggs

For the pancakes

4 eggs
200 g (7 oz/1½ cups) '00' or plain flour
2 tablespoons olive oil
1 teaspoon salt
400 ml (13 fl oz/1¾ cups) whole milk
sunflower oil, for frying

This is pure comfort food; spirals of pancakes are filled with ham, sausage meat, smoked cheese and ricotta, then cut in half and baked until piping hot. This is traditionally served as a starter in Ravello but I think it is filling enough for a main course. Italian sausages do not contain bread or rusk – if they are unavailable try to use gluten-free or coarse-cut artisan sausages instead. For a vegetarian alternative substitute cooked spinach for the meats.

An Italian lady showed me a trick for frying pancakes: cut a small potato in half and spear the rounded side with a fork. Dip the flat side into sunflower oil in a small bowl and use it to wipe a thin layer of oil around the frying pan. Works brilliantly!

This recipe serves 12 as when I make this I prepare two dishes: one for now and one for the freezer. If freezing, allow to defrost in the fridge overnight then bake in the oven.

Start by making the filling. Heat the oil in a large non-stick frying pan and fry the onion over a medium heat for 5–7 minutes, until soft. Add a twist of black pepper. (Add a little salt later if necessary if the sausages are not too salty.) Cut open the sausages and remove the meat. Crumble the sausage meat into the pan and break it up with a wooden spoon. Cook until browned. Pour in the wine and leave it to reduce for a few minutes. Remove the pan from the heat and spread the meat onto a large plate or tray to cool, then mix in the rest of the filling ingredients.

Meanwhile, make the pancakes. In a bowl, whisk the eggs and flour together and gradually add the remaining ingredients, using an electric whisk or hand-held blender to obtain a very smooth batter. Heat a little sunflower oil in a 25 cm (10 inch) non-stick frying pan and use 5 tablespoons of batter per pancake (you should get 12 pancakes out of the

batter). Fry the pancakes, flipping them over when one side is browned and stack them on a plate as you make them. Lay them out and spread 100 g (3½ oz) filling over each one, leaving a 2 cm (¾ inch) edge all round. Roll them up and cut in half. Generously butter the lasagne dishes and stand each spiral up with the cut side upwards, squashing them down slightly to make them stay upright. Bake for 20–25 minutes, or until golden brown and crisp on top. Remove from the oven and allow to stand for about 10 minutes, or they will be too hot to eat. If you are having these as a main course, try them with sautéed broccoli, chard leaves or spinach.

Pink- and peach-coloured flowers, known as Angels' Trumpets, look down from above. From every windowsill and in pots by the doors basil plants scent the air.

GNOCCHI RIPIENI

SMOKED CHEESE GNOCCHI

Serves 4 (makes 12 large or 20 small gnocchi)

1 quantity of tomato sauce of your choice (pages 97–100)

For the gnocchi
250 g (9 oz) ricotta drained
1 egg
35 g (1¼ oz/¼ cup) '00' or plain flour
50 g (2 oz) Parmesan, finely grated
25 g (1 oz) smoked cheese, such as scamorza or smoked Cheddar, finely grated
salt and freshly ground black pepper
50 g (2 oz/⅓ cup) semolina to serve
basil leaves
Parmesan or Grana Padano shavings

I absolutely love these light little dumplings of smoked cheese and ricotta, which are usually served with a simple tomato sauce. The centre melts, giving the appearance that the gnocchi are stuffed with melted cheese. They are completely different to potato gnocchi.

First prepare your chosen tomato sauce.

Next, mix all the gnocchi ingredients except the semolina together in a bowl, using an electric whisk to achieve a smooth mixture. Bring a large pan of well-salted water to the boil.

If making large gnocchi, use tablespoons; if making small gnocchi, use teaspoons. To shape the gnocchi, use 2 spoons to make quenelles: take a spoonful of the mixture, hold a spoon in each hand and form ovals like small rugby balls by scraping the mixture from one spoon to the other, squeezing it together as you work. Roll the shapes into the semolina to coat them, then drop them in batches into the boiling water. They will float to the surface when cooked. Lift them out gently using a slotted spoon and add them directly to the pan containing the sauce of your choice. Make sure the sauce is warm and gently toss the gnocchi in the sauce to coat. Serve immediately with basil leaves and shavings of Parmesan or Grana Padano.

GNOCCHI
ALLA SORRENTINA

POTATO GNOCCHI WITH TOMATO SAUCE, MOZZARELLA & BASIL

Serves 6

1 kg (2 lb 3 oz) floury potatoes, such as
    King Edward, Maris Piper or
    Desirée
1 heaped teaspoon salt
generous twist of black pepper
300 g (10½/2⅓ cups) '00' flour
1 egg

To serve
Our Favourite or Winter tomato sauce
    (see pages 97–98)
125 g (4 oz) ball mozzarella
fresh basil leaves

Although this dish originates from Sorrento, its comforting combination of soft potato gnocchi, rich red tomato sauce, moon-white mozzarella and aromatic basil is now served all over the Amalfi Coast. These potato gnocchi are also delicious with ragù or the clam sauce from the 'Ndunderi recipe (page 133).

Potatoes that are neither too floury nor too waxy are best used to make gnocchi. Gnocchi freeze really well, uncooked. This can sometimes give a lighter result, so consider doubling the quantities and freezing half. To freeze, spread them out on a well-floured tray so that they are not touching. When frozen, shake off excess flour and transfer to freezer bags, seal and freeze. Use within three months. Cook from frozen, allowing 1–2 minutes extra cooking time.

Boil the potatoes in their skins in plenty of salted water until tender. Although this takes about an hour the flavour is far superior than boiling chopped potatoes and they are less watery. Peel them while they are still hot: hold on a fork in one hand and peel the skin away with a sharp knife. Pass the potatoes through a *passatutto* (food mill) or ricer onto a wooden board.

Add the seasoning and the flour, then the egg, and knead together to form a soft, pliable dough. Bring a large pan of well-salted water to the boil.

Lightly flour your work surface. Roll an apple-sized piece of dough into a 2 cm (¾ inch) thick length. Cut into 2 cm (¾ inch) long pieces with a cook's knife, flicking the gnocchi to one side as you cut them. Repeat until all the dough is used.

Cook the gnocchi in 2 batches. Drop them into the boiling water and cook for about 2 minutes. They will float to the surface when cooked. Lift them out gently, using a slotted spoon, and toss them into the tomato sauce. Serve with the mozzarella torn into pieces and the basil leaves.

GIANFRANCO'S
RICOTTA GNOCCHI 'NDUNDERI

**Serves 4 as a main course or
6 as a starter (makes 30 gnocchi)**

350 g (12 oz) ricotta
150 g (5 oz/1¼ cups) '00' flour
35 g (1¼ oz) Parmesan, finely grated
1 teaspoon salt
pinch of white pepper (optional)

For the sauce
5 tablespoons extra-virgin olive oil
1 courgette (zucchini), cut into
    fine strips
600 g (1lb 5 oz) clams
1 large garlic clove, lightly crushed
freshly ground black pepper
50 ml (2 fl oz/¼ cup) white wine
handful of parsley, roughly chopped

To serve
shavings of pecorino (optional)

These beautifully light ricotta gnocchi are the speciality of Minori. We visited the restaurant Il Giardiniello, where they are made by the owner's mother, to sample them. Here they are served in a rich tomato sauce softened by the smoky provola cheese. Our friend Gianfranco from the Amalfi Coast makes them at his restaurant Zero in Hertfordshire and this is his recipe – minus the eggs – to keep them light. Usually cheese is not served with shellfish, but on the Amalfi Coast they make an exception and I simply love it.

Start by making the gnocchi. Mix the ingredients together in a bowl and knead for a couple of minutes only on a floured work surface. Gianfranco's tip is that the less you work the dough, the better. Roll the dough into long, fat sausages and cut into smaller 4 cm (1½ inch) lengths. Use a ridged board or the side of a grater to roll them into large curls, using three fingertips to push them down. Repeat until the dough is finished and set aside on a floured surface (see images overleaf).

Bring a large pan of well-salted water to the boil. Meanwhile, prepare the sauce. Heat 1 tablespoon of oil in a large frying pan and fry the courgette strips until crispy. Remove from the pan and set aside on kitchen paper to drain.

Heat the remaining oil in the pan and when hot add the clams and garlic, then cover. Shake the pan frequently and cook until all the clams have opened. Discard any that do not open. Pour in the wine and allow the sauce to reduce slightly.

Meanwhile, cook the gnocchi. Drop them into the boiling water and cook for about 3 minutes. They will float to the surface when cooked. Lift them out gently, using a slotted spoon, and toss them into the pan with the clams, along with a tablespoon of cooking water. Add the parsley, and serve in warmed bowls with the shavings of Pecorino.

SCIALATIELLI

FRESH PASTA RIBBONS
WITH HERBS & PARMESAN

**Serves 4 as a main course or
6 as a starter**

500 g (1lb 2 oz/4 cups) '00' flour
35 g (1¼ oz) Parmesan, finely grated
225 ml (8 fl oz/1 cup) whole or
    semi-skimmed milk
1 egg
50 g (2 oz) basil or parsley, finely
    chopped

Scialatielli are a speciality of the Amalfi Coast and are made from dough mixed with either basil for a fish sauce or parsley for a meat-based sauce. They are easy and fun to make and completely satisfying to eat. Try them with basil for the sausage sauce below or with parsley for the clam sauce in the 'Ndunderi recipe on page 133.

Mix the flour and cheese together in a large bowl and make a well in the centre. In a separate bowl, mix the milk and egg together and then add to the flour with the herbs. Use one hand or a dough scraper to blend the ingredients into a rough ball of dough. Turn out and knead on a floured work surface for about 5 minutes until it is smooth and well blended. Discard any dry crumbs that have not blended in. At this point the pasta can be wrapped in clingfilm and kept in the fridge for up to 24 hours.

Roll half the pasta out into an oval shape and push through the thickest setting of a pasta machine. Fold the ends of each strip in and push it through again. Repeat until smooth and about 3 mm (⅛ inch) thick. It should go through the rollers about 7 times. Repeat with the other half.

Cut the pasta sheets into 12 × 9 cm (5 × 3½ inch) rectangles. Flour the pieces well and put these through the tagliatelle cutter on the machine to cut into ribbons. (To do these by hand, use a rolling pin to roll out a length of pasta to the above measurements.) Dust the rectangles with flour and loosely roll up. Cut the roll into 1 cm (½ inch) wide lengths with a cook's knife then separate the strips.

The pasta should be well floured and either frozen in freezer bags or cooked within 10–15 minutes or it will become sticky. Cook in salted boiling water for 3–4 minutes and toss into the sauce to finish cooking for a couple more minutes. If cooking from frozen, allow another minute to cook.

SUGO DI SALSICCIA, PORCINI & PANCETTA

SAUSAGE, PORCINI & BACON SAUCE FOR THE SCIALATIELLI

Serves 4 as a main course or 6 as a starter

2 tablespoons extra-virgin olive oil
200 g (7 oz) Italian sausages
50 g (2 oz) dried porcini, soaked and sliced
50 g (2 oz) smoked pancetta or smoked bacon, cut into strips
2 garlic cloves, lightly crushed
10 cherry tomatoes, quartered
1 quantity of Scialatielli (page 136), to serve

Heat the oil in a large frying pan. Cut open the sausages and remove the meat. Crumble the sausage meat into the pan and break it up with a wooden spoon. Add the porcini, pancetta or bacon and garlic to the pan, and fry until the meat is lightly browned and cooked through. Add the cherry tomatoes and briefly cook until just soft. Cook the scialatielli and combine with the sauce before serving.

PESCE
FISH

There is a local saying that goes: "O'pesc nu chiagne quanno o'pigl, ma quanno o'cuoc!', which translates as 'The fish doesn't cry when it is caught, only when it is cooked!', as if even the fish have certain standards in cooking. On the whole of the Sorrentine Peninsula, it is essential to the locals that the freshness and delicate taste of the fish is preserved. Fish is generally grilled or fried. Here it's all about the fish, not the sauce, as most of the time the fish hasn't travelled more than 50 m (55 yd) from shore to plate.

THE FISH MARKET

The fish market on the road to Agerola is small but very popular. The friendly staff sell to the trade and individual shoppers alike. Here cuttle-fish, calamari and octopus are sold from open boxes alongside all types of local fish brought here by the fishermen.

In the market we watched tattooed fishmongers prepare anchovies. The tiny fish heads were cut off and discarded then the fish were slit open gently from the tail to the top and the spine removed. These would be marinated with lemon or vinegar, garlic and chilli, and then preserved under oil for antipasti.

SPIGOLA
IN CROSTA DI SALE
SEA BASS IN SALT

Serves 2

1 sea bream weighing approximately
375 g (13 oz), cleaned
3 large sprigs of parsley
3 sprigs of thyme
1 bay leaf
3 egg whites
400 g (14 oz) coarse sea salt
a good single-estate extra-virgin
   olive oil, to serve

This is the way Gianpaolo, the chef at Il Pirata in Praiano, cooks his sea bass. He told us that the flavour of this dish should be **molto delicato** *(very delicate) and that it is 'a perfect marriage of the freshest fish and local olive oil'. The salt crust traps the flavour inside. I have made this recipe many times using only salt and water but his method of adding egg white makes the crust much easier to cut away after cooking. For this dish a mixture of herbs such as thyme, bay, parsley and basil is suitable, so long as when chopped they amount to roughly 3 tablespoons.*

Preheat the oven to 180°C (350°F/Gas 4). Fill the cavity of the fish with 2 parsley sprigs, 1 thyme sprig and the bay leaf. Finely chop the rest of the parsley and thyme. Whisk the egg whites until they form stiff peaks and hold their shape. Gently fold the herbs and salt into the egg whites without compromising the airiness of the beaten whites. Put 2 large spoonfuls of the mixture on the base of a baking dish lined with parchment, then lay the fish on top. Spoon the rest of the egg white mixture over until the fish until it is completely covered. Bake in the oven for 20–25 minutes.

   To serve, crack open the crust and remove most of it. Loosen the skin around the sides of the fish with a knife. Put the end of the skin by the tail through the prongs of a fork and roll up to lift it away. Use a fish slice to put the fillets onto warmed plates and drizzle with olive oil.

PESCE ALLA GRIGLIA
FISH ON THE GRILL

On the whole, the Amalfitani don't tend to serve a side with fish. Instead, they drizzle it with locally made olive oil because the flavour of the fish is what's important. However, one idea I loved was to make up an oil infused with mint and lemon.

Take a selection of seafood and brush lightly with olive oil. Season on all sides and cook on a hot grill, skin side down. When the flesh turns opaque around the edges, gently flip over and cook the other side until firm to the touch. Prawns should be pink all over and calamari only take about a minute a side or until they become opaque.

OLIO ALLA MENTA
MINT OIL

handful of mint leaves
100 ml (3½ fl oz/½ cup) extra-virgin
  olive oil
juice of ½ lemon
salt, to taste

The flavour of this zingy oil explodes in your mouth. It is perfect for grilled fish or lamb. Depending on the strength of the mint you may need more leaves. I make small amounts of this oil as it tastes and looks better freshly made.

Put the mint leaves and olive oil in a food processor and whizz until smooth. Alternatively, you can use a pestle and mortar. Add the lemon juice and salt to taste. Sieve through a fine mesh and pour into a small jug to serve. A variation of this oil is to use white wine vinegar instead of lemon juice.

OLIO AL BASILICO
BASIL OIL

20 g (¾ oz) basil leaves
100 ml (3½ fl oz/½ cup) extra-virgin
  olive oil
salt, to taste

Made well basil oil adds beauty, colour and a delicate flavour to many dishes and is often served in restaurants. It will keep at room temperature for a few days but the colour will fade, so make small amounts as it is best served fresh.

Put the basil leaves and olive oil in a food processor and whizz until smooth. Alternatively, you can use a pestle and mortar. Add the salt to taste. Sieve through a fine mesh and pour into a small jug to serve.

CALAMARI & GAMBERI
FRITTI ALLA MARCO

CRISPY BATTERED SQUID & PRAWNS

Serves 4

small handful of parsley
2 sprigs of thyme
10 basil leaves
75 g (2½ oz/⅔ cup) fine semolina
4 calamari, cleaned and cut into 2 cm
   slices, or 500 g (1lb 6 oz) mixed
   seafood
juice of 1 lemon, plus 1 lemon cut into
   wedges, to serve
salt and freshly ground black pepper
sunflower oil, for deep frying
handful of rocket leaves, to serve
1 tablespoon extra-virgin olive oil

Marco di Simone, our sous chef at Caldesi in Campagna originates from Naples and this is his favourite way to serve fried calamari. The same can be done with prawns (shrimp) and small fish such as whitebait, anchovies or sprats. The fish should be cleaned and prepared before dipping in the semolina coating. I love the crunch before you bite into the soft calamari underneath.

Finely chop the herbs together on a board. Transfer to a bowl and stir in the semolina. Soak the calamari, and prawns or fish in the lemon juice and seasoning for 2 minutes, then dunk in the semolina and herb mixture. Heat the oil in a pan or deep-fat fryer until it reaches 175°C (347°F), or a piece of bread sizzles and quickly becomes golden brown. Fry the seafood in batches until golden brown. Remove and drain on kitchen paper. Scatter with a little more salt.

Dress the rocket leaves with the olive oil and divide into serving bowls. Lay the seafood on top and serve with lemon wedges.

Row upon row of lemon groves cover the steep mountains surrounding Ravello. Hazy mountain tops fade into the clouds.

PESCE ALL'ACQUA PAZZA

FISH IN CRAZY WATER

Serves 4

4 garlic cloves
2 whole small sea bream or 1 large sea
   bass, cleaned and deboned
salt and freshly ground black pepper
'00' or plain flour, to coat the fish
6 tablespoons olive oil
½ red chilli, depending on strength,
   finely chopped
20 cherry tomatoes, halved
600 ml (20 fl oz/2½ cups) hot water
   or fish stock
handful of flat-leaf parsley, roughly
   chopped

This dish is all about the fish! I can't emphasize this enough. It's about getting a really fresh fish, cooking it simply and quickly, and enjoying its flavour. The water is turned 'crazy' with the addition of tomatoes, chilli and salt. A friend of ours told us that when eating out, she'll ask if wine is used in the sauce, and if so, she will simply eat elsewhere! In her opinion even the addition of chilli is a step too far; she feels that **acqua pazza** *should contain only garlic, salt and black pepper, olive oil, parsley and of course the ripest, most flavourful tomatoes you can lay your hands on.*

Now, bearing in mind that the lucky Amalfitani live next door to their very own 24/7 fresh fish counter and the flavours of the tomatoes grown around Vesuvio are really strong, I think it's fair to make some allowances. I live inland and as far from any sea as you can get in the UK, so if I want to eat a dish like this I would recommend adding a good splash of homemade Shellfish Stock (see page 73) in place of the water.

Put 1 whole clove of garlic inside the cavity of each fish and finely slice the other cloves for the sauce. Season and flour the fish and tap off the excess flour. Heat half the oil in a frying pan and fry the fish for about 5 minutes on each side, remove the fish, then discard the oil from the pan. Add the remaining oil to the pan and fry the sliced garlic, chilli and cherry tomatoes for 2 minutes, making sure that the garlic doesn't burn. Add the hot water or fish stock and bring to the boil. Allow it to boil viciously until the liquor reduces. Garnish with the parsley and serve immediately.

SPIGOLA AL FORNO

BAKED WILD SEA BASS

Serves 4-6

1 large sea bass or sea bream
    (weighing approximately
    1 kg/2 lb 3 oz)
1 lemon, cut into slices
handful of parsley
salt
extra-virgin olive oil

Bass or bream will work equally well here, just so long as it is as fresh as possible. This dish is really about the flavour of the fish with a little disguise in the form of a sauce. I serve it with salad and bread in summer and spinach and potatoes in winter.

Preheat the oven to 180°C (350°F/Gas 4). Lay the sea bass on a large greased ovenproof dish. Put most of the lemon slices in the cavity, along with the parsley and some salt. Scatter a little more salt over the top of the fish and drizzle with olive oil. Lay a few more slices of lemon on top and bake in the oven for 35 minutes. To check if the fish is done, insert a thermometer with a probe: the internal temperature should read 60°C (140°F). If you do not have a thermometer, press the top of the fish with your fingers: it should feel firm to the touch. You can also slide a knife near the backbone and give it a twist: if it lifts and the flesh easily comes away from the backbone the fish is done.

TOTANI & PATATE

RED CALAMARI & FRIED POTATOES

Serves 4 as a main course or 6 as a starter

2 large calamari, cleaned but including tentacles
6 tablespoons extra-virgin olive oil
1 red onion, finely chopped
1 large garlic clove, finely chopped
200 g (7 oz) potatoes, peeled and cut into 1 cm (½ inch) thick half-moon shapes
generous pinch of salt
½–1 red chilli, depending on strength, thinly sliced
1 heaped tablespoon finely chopped parsley

*This is the speciality dish of Praiano, where **totani**, or red calamari, are collected in the evenings. They are a local variety of squid with a reddish hue to their speckled skin. Ask your fishmonger to clean the calamari for you as it's quite a tricky, never mind messy, job if you haven't done it before.*

Cut the calamari in half lengthways and then into 2 cm (¾ inch) wide strips. Slice the tentacles into bite-size pieces. Heat half the oil in a frying pan and sauté the onion and garlic together. When just soft, add the calamari and cook for 5 minutes, stirring and shaking the pan frequently.

Meanwhile, heat the remaining oil in a separate frying pan and fry the potatoes for 2–3 minutes. Remove from the pan with a slotted spoon and add to the calamari and onions. Add a good pinch of salt, the chilli and the parsley and reduce the heat to minimum. Shake the pan gently for 1–2 minutes so that the water from the calamari is absorbed by the potatoes. Taste and adjust the seasoning if necessary before serving.

IMPEPATA DI COZZE
PEPPERED MUSSELS

Serves 6 as a starter

1 kg (2 lb 3 oz) mussels, cleaned and
   debearded
½ teaspoon freshly ground black
   pepper
50 ml (2 fl oz/¼ cup) water
juice of 1 lemon, plus 1 lemon cut into
   slices, to serve
parsley, to garnish

*Our fiend Rino runs Il Pirata, a restaurant perched on the
edge of a rock cliff with the beautiful sea below. We loved
eating there. While sipping chilled Falanghina we pinched
out plump juicy mussels from their shells and watched the
staff cast luminous flies into the water to catch fish at the end
of the evening service.*

Put the mussels in a large frying pan with the black pepper.
Place over a medium heat and add water. Cover and cook,
shaking the pan frequently. When the last mussel opens
add the lemon juice and serve with the lemon slices. Discard
any unopened shells.

POLLAME
& CARNE

POULTRY
& MEAT

Near misses every two minutes make bus and car journeys exciting to say the least. After a while nerves turn to laughter at the audacity of the Amalfitani drivers.

Meat takes a backseat to the local fish dishes and this is perhaps where Amalfi cooking differs most from that of its neighbouring Naples. There simply isn't the space or terrain for herds of cattle. However, though not numerous, the meat dishes of the region are delicious nonetheless. Beef usually ends up in various permutations of ragù, and though steak is widely available, it is mainly ordered by tourists. It is common for the locals to breed chickens and rabbits for their own personal use, and game birds are hunted in the hills, along with wild rabbits. As for sheep, they graze in the valleys and are used for their milk as well as their meat.

Rufolo

mare

i 20

MACELLERIA

CAMERA

VILLA CIMBRONE

VILLA CIMBRONE

POLPETTINE DI CARNE
AL SUGO DI POMODORO

MEATBALLS IN TOMATO SAUCE

Serves 6 (makes 20–24 meatballs)

75 g (2½ oz/generous ½ cup)
   sultanas
200 g (7 oz) stale white rustic bread,
   crusts removed
500 ml (17 fl oz/generous 2 cups) milk
small handful of parsley
2 garlic cloves
500 g (1lb 2 oz) minced ground beef,
   or half beef and half pork
salt and freshly ground black pepper
2 eggs
40 g (1½ oz/¼ cup) pine nuts
100 g (3½ oz) Grana Padano,
   finely grated
5 tablespoons sunflower oil
'00' or plain flour, to coat the
   meatballs
1 quantity of tomato sauce
   (made with 2 × 400 g/14 oz cans
   tomatoes, see pages 97–98)

The quantities in this recipe make a large portion of meat-balls. They are perfect for freezing so we usually make a big batch and freeze half.

Soak the sultanas in warm water and the bread in milk for 10 minutes while you prepare the rest of the ingredients. Finely chop the parsley and garlic together, using a large knife. Transfer to a bowl with the meat, seasoning, eggs, pine nuts and grated cheese. Drain the sultanas and add these to the bowl. Squeeze the bread and discard the milk, then break it up into very small pieces and add it to the bowl. Use your hands to mix the ingredients together.

Wet your hands and shape the mixture into meatballs the shape of rugby balls measuring approximately 7 × 4 cm (2¾ × 1½ inches). Lay them on a tray while you complete the task.

Heat the oil in a large frying pan. Coat the meatballs in flour and tap off the excess. Fry the balls in batches in the hot oil until lightly browned all over. They will cook further in the tomato sauce, so do not worry about them not being cooked through. Once browned, remove them from the pan with a slotted spoon and drain on kitchen paper.

Discard the oil from the pan and make the tomato sauce, following one of the recipes on pages 97–98. Add the meat-balls to the sauce and cook for about 30 minutes over a low to medium heat until the meat is cooked through (test by cutting into a meatball: the inside should be brown and not red). The Italians would eat this with bread, followed by a salad for afterwards.

CONIGLIO ALL'ISCHITANA

RABBIT FROM ISCHIA

Serves 6

1 rabbit, jointed, skin left on
salt and freshly ground black pepper
'00' or plain flour, to coat the rabbit
4 tablespoons sunflower oil
6 tablespoons extra-virgin olive oil
1 fresh red chilli, finely sliced
2 garlic cloves, lightly crushed
2 long sprigs of rosemary
200 ml (7 fl oz/1 scant cup) white wine
400 g (14 oz/2 cups) cherry or ripe
    round tomatoes, or 400 g (14 oz)
    can plum tomatoes
500 ml (17 fl oz/generous 2 cups)
    hot chicken or rich vegetable stock
80 g (3 oz/½ cup) good-quality black
    olives
handful of parsley, roughly chopped
Enza's fried potatoes (see page 186)
    and sautéed chard leaves or
    spinach, to serve

This is said to be the way the people from the small island of Ischia, off the coast of Naples, cook wild rabbit. Invest in good-quality olives, such as taggiasche or kalamata bought with stones in and remove just before cooking. The flavour will greatly improve the dish.

Season the pieces of rabbit with salt and black pepper. Coat the pieces in flour and tap off the excess. A quick way of doing this is to put the flour into a plastic food bag with the rabbit pieces and shake the bag, making sure the meat is evenly coated.

Heat the sunflower oil in a pan and fry the rabbit until golden-brown and crispy. Be patient, as the crispier and more golden the skin, the more flavour it will create. Remove the rabbit from the pan, pour away the oil and clean off any very burnt bits from the pan – brown is good, blackened is not.

Heat the olive oil in the pan and fry the chilli, garlic and rosemary for 1 minute. Put the rabbit back into the pan and pour in the wine. Allow the wine to evaporate (this will take a couple of minutes) then add the tomatoes and stir through. Pour in the hot stock, add the olives and cook for 1½ hours, or until the rabbit is really tender and falls off the bone. Stir in the parsley and serve with fried potatoes and sautéed chard leaves or spinach.

When rough seas deter the fishermen and the weather cools, the Amalfitani turn to the mountains above for their catch.

POLLO ALLA CACCIATORA

HUNTER'S CHICKEN

Serves 6

1 free-range chicken, jointed
salt and freshly ground black pepper
'00' or plain flour, to coat the chicken
sunflower oil, to brown the chicken
2 sprigs of rosemary
3 garlic cloves
2 slices unsmoked bacon or pancetta
5 tablespoons extra-virgin olive oil
2 red bell peppers, roughly chopped
2 large potatoes, peeled and chopped
   into large bite-size pieces
175 ml (6 fl oz/¾ cup) white wine
2 tablespoons tomato purée
400 g (14 oz) can plum tomatoes
100 g (3½ oz/⅔ cup) good-quality
   black olives, stoned
400 ml (13 fl oz/1¾ cups) water
1 tablespoon roughly chopped parsley
fresh crusty bread, to serve

Do be fussy in your choice of olives; the flavour is so much better if you buy them with stones in and remove them just before cooking. Good-quality black kalamata or taggiasche are best for this dish. To remove the stones, squash them with the blade of a knife and the stones will pop out. As this dish is really based on whatever the hunter's catch of the day is, it works equally well with rabbit or guinea fowl.

Season the pieces of chicken with salt and black pepper. Coat in flour and tap off the excess. A quick way of doing this is to put the flour in a plastic food bag with the chicken pieces and shake the bag, making sure the meat is evenly coated. Heat the sunflower oil in a pan and brown the chicken very well all over. Remove the chicken from the pan and pour away the oil.

Finely chop the rosemary, garlic and bacon or pancetta together. Heat the olive oil in the pan and fry the rosemary, garlic and bacon for just 1 minute, taking care not to burn the mixture, before adding the peppers and potatoes. Cook for 2 minutes and then return the chicken pieces to the pan. When hot, pour in the wine and allow it to evaporate for 2 minutes before adding the tomato purée, tomatoes, olives and cold water. Break up the tomatoes with a wooden spoon. Partially cover the chicken and cook for about 1 hour, or until the meat falls off the bones. Stir in the parsley and serve with hunks of bread to mop up the juices and a green salad.

POLLO
AL LIMONE
LEMON CHICKEN

Serves 4

8 boneless chicken thighs, skin on
salt and freshly ground black pepper
'00' or plain flour, to coat the chicken
1 tablespoon olive oil
2 garlic cloves, lightly crushed
3 small sprigs of rosemary
100 ml (3½ fl oz/½ cup) white wine
50 ml (2 fl oz/¼ cup) water
juice of 1 lemon (reserve the juiced
  halves)
25 g (1 oz/2 tablespoons) butter
new or fried potatoes to serve
slices of lemon to garnish

Chicken thighs are underused, in my opinion. They are economical, succulent, full of flavour (more so than the overused breast) and cook quickly. This simple recipe is great as a quick supper dish.

Season the pieces of chicken with salt and black pepper. Coat the pieces in flour and tap off the excess. A quick way of doing this is to put the flour in a plastic food bag with the chicken pieces and shake the bag, making sure the meat is evenly coated.

Heat the oil in a non-stick frying pan and fry the chicken skin-side down first until golden brown. Turn the chicken over and brown the other side, adding the garlic and rosemary. Pour away the excess oil and return to the heat.

Pour in the wine and allow it to reduce for a few minutes, then add water, lemon juice and butter. Add the lemon halves to the pan and keep on the heat until the chicken is cooked through. Discard the lemon halves and serve with new or fried potatoes.

AGNELLO ALLA GRIGLIA
CON SALSA DI ALICI

LAMB ON THE GRILL
WITH ANCHOVY DRESSING

Serves 4

For the lamb

12 lamb cutlets
3 tablespoons extra-virgin olive oil
3 garlic cloves, lightly crushed
2 sprigs of rosemary
salt and freshly ground black pepper

For the dressing

6 anchovy fillets in oil
1 large garlic clove
handful of parsley
generous twist of freshly ground
    black pepper
6–8 tablespoons extra-virgin olive oil

This is great cooked on a barbecue where the flavour of the lamb is enhanced by the charcoal. It is such a quick and easy recipe it has become one of our favourites for summer barbecues. It's great with fried potatoes or crusty focaccia and salad.

Start by preparing the lamb. Marinate it in a plastic food bag with the olive oil, garlic, rosemary and seasoning for at least 1 hour and up to a day in the fridge.

To make the dressing, finely chop the anchovies, garlic and parsley together on a chopping board. Scrape into a bowl and stir in the black pepper and olive oil a little at a time to obtain a thick sauce.

Cook the lamb to your liking on a grill or barbecue. Transfer to a serving dish with the dressing on the side.

CONTORNI

VEGETABLES

Vegetables are often combined with beans or pasta to make up a meal in place of meat. If you are vegetarian you might not find a vegetarian main course aside from pasta but try combining a few of the **contorni**, or side dishes, that are often delicious in their own right. Salad as a main course doesn't really exist in Italy, which may seem strange given its climate and produce. Cooked vegetables are the order of the day throughout the year. One of my favourites is **friarielli**, belonging to the broccoli family. It is often boiled then fried with sausages. I could eat tonnes of it, but sadly it seems unavailable outside the region of Campania. Broccoli and cauliflower are sometimes eaten cold drizzled with lemon juice and oil. Bitter greens, such as escarole, are popular as a topping for pizza or boiled and fried as a side order.

In Amalfi, sun-drenched tomatoes are eaten for flavour, not their good looks... and wow, what a flavour!

Slow-Roasted Florence Fennel
with Thyme

PATATE DI ENZA

ENZA'S FRIED POTATOES

Serves 4-6

200–300ml (7–10 fl oz/scant 1–1¼ cups)
  sunflower oil, for frying (add more
  if necessary)
600 g (1 lb 5 oz) floury potatoes such
  as Maris Piper or King Edwards,
  unpeeled
1 white onion
salt

This simple dish goes with almost everything and is quick to make. Leave out the onion if you wish, and if serving with meat throw in some rosemary at the end.

Heat the oil in a deep-sided frying pan until it reaches 175°C (347°F), or a piece of bread sizzles and quickly becomes golden brown. Slice the potatoes and onions lengthways and then into 5 mm (¼ inch) half moons. Fry the potatoes until just golden brown, then add the onions and continue to cook until crisp. Drain on kitchen paper and transfer to a warmed serving dish. Scatter with salt before serving.

FINOCCHIO
AL FORNO CON TIMO

SLOW-ROASTED
FLORENCE FENNEL WITH THYME

Serves 4

3 whole fennel bulbs
3 tablespoons extra-virgin olive oil
salt and freshly ground black pepper
125 ml (4¼ fl oz/½ cup) white wine
1 tablespoon roughly chopped fresh
   thyme leaves

There are two types of fennel: one with a white and pale green bulb, known as Florence fennel and very popular throughout Italy, and wild fennel. The wild variety has small yellow flowers that are collected for their seeds. All parts of the fennel are edible: the seeds are fabulous rubbed into pork belly, the fine fronds are perfect for a new potato salad served with fish, and the soft stems and fronds are used for flavouring pasta dishes and fish.

Preheat the oven to 180°C (350°F/Gas 4). Cut the fennel into 2 cm (¾ inch) slices from root to fronds. Lay in a roasting tray and drizzle with the olive oil. Season generously with salt and black pepper and toss to combine. Cook for 30 minutes, then remove from the oven, pour the wine over and add the thyme. Toss again and cook for a further 30 minutes, or until the fennel is soft and lightly golden.

ZUCCHINE SCAPECE

FRIED COURGETTES
WITH MINT AND VINEGAR

Serves 6

4 courgettes (zucchini)
3 tablespoons extra-virgin olive oil
2 large garlic cloves, lightly crushed
salt and freshly ground black pepper
1–2 tablespoons white wine vinegar
12 mint leaves

Scapece *is from the Spanish word* **escabeche***, left over from the days of Spanish occupation in the area. It means 'dressed with vinegar'. For a lower-fat version of this recipe try steaming the courgettes (zucchini) instead of frying them.*

Slice the courgettes into 1 cm (½ inch) rounds. Heat the oil in a large frying pan and fry the courgettes with the garlic, seasoning the rounds on both sides and cooking until golden brown (if the garlic browns too much discard it). Using a slotted spoon, remove the courgette rounds and lay them on a plate. Drizzle with the vinegar and taste for seasoning. Tear the mint leaves, scattering them over the courgettes. Serve immediately or allow to cool to room temperature before serving.

INSALATA DI PATATE NOVELLE
NEW POTATO & LEMON SALAD

Serves 6

1 kg (2 lb 3 oz) new potatoes
1 tablespoon roughly chopped parsley
juice of ½ lemon
3 tablespoons top-quality extra-virgin
    olive oil
salt and freshly ground black pepper

This is the time to get out that single-estate bottle of olive oil you have been saving! It will make all the difference to this delicious summery potato salad.

Boil the potatoes whole in their skins until tender. This takes longer than if you cut them in half but the flavour is better and the skins will rub off easily after cooking. Combine the remaining ingredients in a small jug to make the dressing. When the potatoes are tender (test by poking a couple with a sharp knife), drain them and allow to cool for 5 minutes. Hold them with a fork and peel off the skins with a small knife or simply rub the skins off with your fingers if you can stand the heat! Crush the potatoes slightly between your fingers and drop into a mixing bowl. Pour the dressing over and serve.

INSALATA DI FAGIOLINI
GREEN BEAN SALAD

Serves 4

½ white or red onion
300 g (10 oz) runner, flat or
    green beans
2 tablespoons extra-virgin olive oil
2 teaspoons white wine vinegar
salt and freshly ground black pepper

Italians prefer beans to be cooked until soft rather than squeaky and crisp. I have got used to this now and enjoy their flavour more than ever. Any type of green bean works for this recipe.

Slice the onion in half and then into thin semi-circles. Soak in a bowl of cold water for 10 minutes to remove some of their strength. Cook the beans in salted water for about 10 minutes, or until tender. Drain and then toss with the onion, olive oil and vinegar. Season to taste and serve at room temperature.

BIETOLE IN DUE VERSIONI
RAINBOW CHARD IN TWO WAYS

Serves 4-6

650 g (1 lb 7 oz) chard stems, chopped
    into 3 cm (1 inch) lengths
4 tablespoons olive oil
juice of ½ lemon
2 garlic cloves, finely chopped
salt and freshly ground black pepper

SAUTEED CHARD LEAVES WITH CHILLI & GARLIC
Chard, a relative of the beet family, was widely cultivated by the Greeks and Romans. The leaves and stems can both be eaten but should be prepared separately because of their different cooking times.

Boil or steam the chard stems for 10 to 15 minutes until tender. Drain in a colander and transfer to a serving dish. Add the olive oil, lemon juice and garlic, and season to taste. Serve at room temperature.

VARIATIONS
You can replace the chard leaves with spinach, sliced courgettes (zucchini), shredded cabbage or Brussels sprouts.

Serves 4

650 g (1 lb 7 oz) chard stems, chopped
    into 3cm (1 inch) lengths
1 white onion, finely chopped
2 garlic cloves, lightly crushed
3 tablespoons extra-virgin olive oil
50g (2 oz) black or purple olives,
    pitted and roughly chopped
vegetable stock, as necessary
200 g (7 oz) canned chopped Italian
    plum tomatoes (about half a can)
    or the juice of one lemon
salt and freshly ground black pepper,
    to taste

CHARD STEMS WITH TOMATOES & OLIVES
This recipe uses tomatoes but chard is also good with lemon juice instead – both the tomato and the lemon offer acidity to the end dish.

Chop the stems into small cubes and cook in plenty of boiling salted water for 15 minutes. Drain.

Fry the onion and garlic, salt and pepper in the olive oil in a large frying pan until just soft. Add the olives and the boiled stems and stir to combine. Stir in the tomatoes or lemon juice and heat through for ten to fifteen minutes. Taste and adjust seasoning as necessary.

Clockwise, from right: Chard Stems with Tomatoes; New Potato & Lemon Salad; Sautéed Chard Leaves; and, Green Bean Salad.

DOLCI
DESSERTS

Tempting cakes and pastries line the shelves of glass cabinets in glamorous old caffés, seducing you to enter.

Of all the regions of Italy, Sicily and Campania have to take first and second places for the best patisserie. Surrounded by lemon groves, almond and walnut trees, and with the influence of Arab trade in the Middle Ages, the Amalfi Coast boasts some of the best cakes and tarts in the country. And that is not counting ice cream and **granita**, a type of frozen sorbet served in a glass, sold on every street corner.

Candied fruits are made in this area and there is no better place to see them than in the windows of Pasticceria Pansa in Amalfi – try their espresso with lemon zest while eating a wonderful **delizia al limone**.

In Minori in 1908 the De Riso family started producing ice creams and granite. In 1989, Salvatore De Riso, opened his patisserie on the **lungomare**, or promenade. This shop-cum-caffé is definitely worth a visit, hosting such a variety of wonderful cakes and pastries. It is particularly famous for its ricotta and pear tart.

Look out for the **sfogliatelle Santa Rosa**, which are strange multi-layered crescents of pastry filled with ricotta and candied fruit. The pastries are made in the shape of the headwear of the nuns who started making them in Conca dei Marini centuries ago.

Around the coast you may come across a strange concoction of chocolate and fried aubergines (eggplants). It is said that the monks from the Franciscan monastery in Tramonti came up this odd combination and originally it was fried aubergines covered with a homemade liqueur. Over the years the liqueur has been replaced with chocolate. We felt it was an acquired taste that was probably best left in Amalfi.

TORTA DI RISO

ARBORIO RICE & CUSTARD TART

**Serves 8–10 (makes one
25 cm/10 inch round cake)**

For the *pasta frolla*
180 g (6¼ oz/¾ cup) salted butter
350 g (12 oz/2¾ cups) '00' or plain
   (all-purpose) flour
135 g (4¾ oz/⅔ cup) caster
   (superfine) sugar
2 eggs

For the filling
200 g (7 oz/scant 1 cup) arborio
   risotto rice or pudding rice
1 litre (34 fl oz/4¼ cups) milk
zest of 1 lemon
1 teaspoon vanilla extract, or seeds
   from a vanilla pod
250 g (9 oz/1 cup) ricotta
250 g (9 oz/1 cup) caster
   (superfine) sugar
125 g (4 oz/1/2 cup) candied fruit, such
   as orange and lemon
1 teaspooon cinnamon powder
4 egg yolks
a few drops of orange flower water
   (optional)

*This tart is based on the traditional **pastiera** cake that was eaten at Easter but has now become available almost all year round. This version is made with rice rather than **grano cotto**, swollen grains of wheat, available pre-cooked in Italian delis. The tart usually contains orange flower water which is a very powerful flavour, so use sparingly if at all.*

Preheat the oven to 180°C (350°F/Gas 4). Start by making the *pasta frolla*. In a bowl, rub the butter and flour together with your fingertips, then use a dough scraper or spatula to mix in the sugar and eggs. When well blended, shape the pastry into a flattened ball, wrap in clingfilm and allow to rest in the fridge while you prepare the rest of the tart.

Generously butter a 3.5 cm (1½ inch) deep, 25 cm (10 inch) round loose-bottomed tin. Peel a strip of zest from the lemon and then grate the remaining zest and reserve for later. Cook the rice in the milk until soft and tender with the strip of zest and half the vanilla – this should take 20–25 minutes. Remove the saucepan from the heat and tip the rice onto a tray to cool, spreading it out thinly so that it cools quickly – the rice needs to cool within 1 hour of cooking to prevent bacterial growth.

Meanwhile, on a floured work surface, roll the pastry out to a circle large enough to line the base and sides of the tin – about 32 cm (12½ inches) in diameter. Line the buttered tin with the pastry and trim the edges with a sharp knife. When the rice is at room temperature, transfer it to a bowl and mix in the remaining filling ingredients, including the reserved grated lemon zest. Pour into the lined tin. Cook for 50–60 minutes, or until the top of the cake is firm to the touch and pale golden. Take out of the oven and remove the outer rim of the tin. Allow to reach room temperature before serving. Store in the fridge if not eaten on the day.

Pausing for a coffee we watched buses speed around the bends, jostling for space on the narrow roads.

DOLCE DI AMALFI
LEMON CAKE

**Serves 8–10 (makes one
25 cm/10 inch ring-shaped cake)**

100 g (3½ oz/⅔ cup) whole almonds
200 g (7 oz/¾ cup) salted butter,
    softened, plus extra for greasing
250 g (9 oz/1⅛ cups) caster
    (superfine) sugar
3 eggs
100 ml (3½ fl oz/1 cup) milk
150 g (5 oz/1¼ cups) '00' or plain flour
zest of 4 lemons, finely grated
1 teaspoon vanilla extract, or seeds
    from a vanilla pod
2 heaped teaspoons baking powder

This is the Amalfi version of a Victoria sponge cake. Do buy whole almonds rather than almond flour as this has the oil stripped out of it and makes a drier cake.

Preheat the oven to 180°C (350°F/Gas 4). Butter the tin. Toast the almonds on a baking tray in the oven for 8–10 minutes, or until pale golden. Remove from the oven and allow to cool a little before blitzing to a powder in a food processor.

In a bowl, cream together the butter and sugar with an electric whisk until light and fluffy. Add the eggs and continue whisking. Fold or whisk in the remaining ingredients. Pour into the prepared cake tin and bake for 40–45 minutes, or until a metal skewer inserted into the cake comes out clean. Leave to cool for a few minutes before turning out onto a wire rack to cool completely.

BABÀ AL RUM
RUM BABA

Makes 8

For the dough
80 ml (2½ fl oz/⅓ cup) milk
25 g (⁹⁄₁₀ oz) fresh yeast or 12 g
   (½ oz) dried yeast
250 g (9 oz/2 cups) strong white flour
pinch of salt
20 g (¾ oz/1½) caster (superfine)
sugar
3 eggs
100 g (3½ oz/⅓ cup) butter,
   softened, plus extra for greasing

For the syrup
300 ml (10 fl oz/1¼ cups) dark rum
300 g (10½ g/1⅓ cups) caster
   (superfine) sugar
300 ml (10 fl oz/1¼ cups) water

If you wanted to tell someone they were sweet you could say in Neapolitan 'Si nu' baba', such is the love Neapolitans have for sweet treats. These small cakes were so called by the exiled King of Poland, Stanislas Leszczynski, after his favourite story Ali Baba and the Arabian Nights. Baba, pronounced bubbà, not barbar, are found in most bars and restaurants in Naples and the Amalfi Coast. Probably not the prettiest cakes on the shelf – they usually look like oversized mushrooms split in two, piped with thick yellow custard and topped with a glacé cherry – they are delicious nonetheless. I like the fact that you can make the baba, syrup and custard the day before and finish them off quickly for a dinner party. Use good-quality dark rum rather than rum essence, as this will make the difference between a good and poor version of baba. The soaking liquid can be kept in the fridge for a week. Miniature versions of baba are also sold soaked in limoncello syrup instead of rum and squeezed into glass jars. For children, make a non-alcoholic syrup using 500 ml (17 fl oz/generous 2 cups) water and 200 g (7 oz/scant 1 cup) caster (superfine) sugar flavoured with a few strips of orange peel.

The photograph shows the baba served at Villa Cimbrone in Ravello on a soup of crème Anglaise with pistachio nuts, silver sugar, rose petals, mint and jam.

Start by making the dough. Heat the milk in a saucepan until tepid and stir in the yeast with a spatula or your fingers, blending it in well. Put the flour, salt and sugar in a bowl and add the eggs and yeasted milk. Mix with an electric mixer or food processor. Add the softened butter as you whisk and beat for about 5 minutes until smooth. Leave to rise in the bowl until doubled in volume. Meanwhile, grease 8 dariole moulds with butter.

When the dough has doubled in size spoon it evenly into eight 7 cm (2¾ inch) deep and 5 cm (2 inch) wide dariole moulds, filling them to two-thirds full. Leave to rise again until the dough rises above the moulds and springs back to the touch; this will take 30–60minutes. Meanwhile, preheat the oven to 180°C (350°F/Gas 4).

Bake for 12–15 minutes, or until golden brown, well risen and cooked through. Remove from the oven and loosen the babas from their mould by running the blade of a knife around the inside of the moulds. Tip onto a wire rack. These can now be frozen and soaked at a later time.

To make the syrup, bring all the ingredients to the boil and then remove from the heat. Stand the babas on a wire rack over a clean tray. Use a skewer to make about 12 long, thin holes in each one. Carefully spoon over the syrup until the babas are soaked through. Serve with custard (see recipe on page 215, but halve the ingredients) and preserved fruits in alcohol, such as cherries.

PAN DI SPAGNA
SPONGE CAKE

Serves 8 (makes one 20 cm/8 inch round cake or 8 smaller cakes)

125 g (4 oz/½ cup) golden caster (superfine) sugar
4 eggs
seeds from a vanilla pod, or 1 teaspoon vanilla extract
finely grated zest of ½ orange (optional)
125 g (4 oz/½ cup) '00' or plain flour
60 g (2 oz/½ stick) salted butter, melted, plus extra for greasing

At Andrea Pansa, the lovely old patisserie that graces the main piazza in Amalfi, long fingers of sponge wrapped in paper are served, ready to be dunked into your breakfast coffee or after-dinner limoncello. The name translates as 'bread of Spain', presumably a recipe left over from the days of Spanish rule.

Preheat the oven to 180°C (350°F/Gas 4). Grease and flour either a 20 cm (8 inch) round tin or 8 semi-spherical moulds measuring 8 cm (3 inch) in diameter and 4 cm (1½ inch) deep, tapping out any excess flour. When the oven is hot, sprinkle the sugar on a baking tray lined with baking parchment and heat in the oven for 5 minutes.

Whisk the eggs in a large bowl for 1 minute, using an electric mixer. Pour in the warm sugar and continue to whisk, adding the vanilla and orange zest, if using, until it leaves a ribbon trail on the surface. To check you've whisked enough, turn off the mixer and make a circle with the beaters over the bowl; the mixture should sit on the surface before sinking in. If there is no trail, continue to whisk. When ready, sift the flour into the bowl and gently fold in. Mix in the melted butter. Pour the mixture into the prepared tin or moulds and smooth the surface.

Bake in the oven for 25-30 minutes for the large cake 15-20 minutes for the smaller cakes, or until golden brown and a metal skewer inserted into the cake(s) comes out clean. Remove from the oven and turn out onto a wire rack.

For the lemon curd

40 g (1½ oz/3 tablespoons) golden
  caster (superfine) sugar
40 g (1½ oz/2½ tablespoons)
  unsalted butter
juice and finely grated zest of 1 lemon
2 egg yolks

For the custard

250 ml (8½ fl oz/generous 1 cup) milk
seeds from ½ vanilla pod
4 egg yolks
finely grated zest of 1 lemon
75 g (2½ oz/⅓ cup) caster (superfine)
  sugar
20 g (¾ oz/3 tablespoons) cornflour
  (cornstarch)

For the lemon syrup

100 ml (3½ fl oz/½ cup) limoncello
100 g (3½ oz/⅜ cup) golden caster
  (superfine) sugar
finely grated zest and juice of 1 lemon
100 ml (3½ fl oz/½ cup) water

For the sponge domes

1 quantity of Pan di Spagna recipe
  batter (see page 209) baked in
  8 semi-spherical moulds measuring
  8 cm (3¼ inches) in diameter and
  4 cm (1½ inches) deep, or 8
  ovenproof cappuccino cups
150 ml (5 fl oz/scant ¾ cup) whipping
  cream
30 g (1 oz/2 tablespoons) golden
  caster sugar
80–100 ml (2½–3½ fl oz/¼–½ cup)
  milk

DELIZIA AL LIMONE

LEMON DOMES
FILLED WITH LEMON CREAM

*Bubbles of air in the sponge and the lemon-scented cream
make this dessert heavenly.*

Start by making the lemon curd. Put the sugar, butter and
lemon juice and zest in a small saucepan. Bring to the boil
and stir constantly, then remove from the heat. Add the egg
yolks and keep stirring until the mixture has thickened.
Transfer to a bowl and cover the surface with clingfilm to
avoid a skin forming.

To make the custard, heat the milk with the vanilla in a
medium saucepan until warm. In a bowl, whisk together the
egg yolks, lemon zest, sugar and cornflour. Whisk in a little
of the warmed milk and then pour this mixture into the
saucepan with the rest of the milk. Stir with a wooden spoon
until the mixture thickens, then remove from the heat.
Transfer to a bowl and cover the surface with clingfilm to
avoid a skin forming. Allow to cool.

To make the lemon syrup, boil all the ingredients together
in a small saucepan for a couple of minutes and then leave
to cool.

Make the sponge domes following the Pan di Spagna
recipe on page 207. Place the domes on a wire rack flat side
up, prick the surface with a cocktail stick and brush with
half the lemon syrup. Turn them over and repeat on the
other side.

In a bowl, mix the lemon curd and custard together. In a separate bowl, whisk the whipping cream and sugar together to form soft peaks and fold this into the lemon curd and custard mixture. Put the mixture into a piping bag and use the tip of the nozzle to make a small hole in the base of the domes and fill with the cream. Transfer the remaining cream into a bowl and mix with the milk so that it becomes the consistency of runny custard. Turn the filled domes rounded side up and lay on a wire rack. Drizzle over the remaining lemon syrup to moisten the sponge. Pour the rest of the loosened cream over the domes to cover them.

Decorate them as you wish, with a few more curls of lemon zest or whipped cream.

TORTA DI RICOTTA & PERE

PEAR & RICOTTA TART

Serves 6–8 (makes one 20 cm/8 inch round cake)

For the sponge
100 g (3½ oz/¾ cup) hazelnuts
50 g (2 oz/⅓ cup) '00' or plain flour
100 g (3½ oz/⅜ cup) caster (superfine) sugar
75 g (2½ oz/⅔ stick) unsalted butter, cut into 4 pieces, plus extra for greasing
4 egg whites
icing (confectioner's) sugar, for dusting

For the filling
2–3 pears (approx 400 g/14 oz), peeled and cut into bite-size pieces
75 ml (2½ fl oz/¼ cup) water
1 vanilla pod, split lengthways in two, or 1 teaspoon vanilla extract
125 g (4 oz/⅝ cup) golden caster (superfine) sugar
250 g (9 oz/1 cup) ricotta, drained
100 g (3½ fl oz/½ cup) double cream

Crumbly white ricotta is sandwiched between layers of soft, sweet pears and a dark hazelnut sponge. It is perfectly balanced in flavours and textures – hence its success. This dessert was made famous by Sal De Riso, the fantastic patisserie in Minori. In their version the pears are cooked in rum.

Grease two 20 cm (8 inch) round tins with butter and line the bottoms with baking parchment. Preheat the oven to 180°C (350°F/Gas 4). Scatter the hazelnuts on a baking tray and toast in the oven for 10 minutes. Remove from the oven and allow to cool but leave the oven on.

Use a food processor to blitz the nuts to a sandy consistency. Add the flour, sugar and butter to the food processor and whizz again to blend. In a large bowl, whisk the egg whites to soft peaks and then fold them into the nut mixture. Pour into the prepared tins and bake for 20 minutes. Remove from the oven and leave to cool for 5 minutes before turning out onto wire racks. Peel off the circles of baking parchment.

To make the filling, cook the pears in the water, together with the vanilla and 75 g (2½ fl oz/⅓ cup) of the sugar in a saucepan until soft, for 15–20 minutes (depending on the ripeness of the pears). This is best done with a circle of baking parchment pressed down on the pears to trap in the steam. When the pears are done, strain them through a sieve resting over a bowl to collect the juices and set aside.

Whisk together the remaining sugar, ricotta and cream in a bowl until smooth and thick. When the pears are cool stir them into the cream. Place one hazelnut sponge on a board and spoon the filling over. Lay the other sponge on top and push down so that the filling oozes out a little. Smooth the sides with the back of a spoon. Sift the icing sugar over the top and transfer to a serving dish or cake stand. Serve in slices with the syrup from the pears.

MIMOSA

**Serves 8–10 (makes one
20 cm/8 inch round cake)**

For the sponge
2 quantities of Pan di Spagna recipe
(see page 209)

For the syrup
100 ml (3½ oz/½ cup) water
100 g (3½ oz/scant ½ cup) caster
(superfine) sugar
50 ml (2 fl oz/¼ cup) Strega liqueur,
Grand Marnier or brandy

For the custard
500 ml (17 fl oz/generous 2 cups) milk
seeds from a vanilla pod, or 1 teaspoon
vanilla extract
3 egg yolks
finely grated zest of 1 lemon
100 g (3½ oz/⅜ cup) caster
(superfine) sugar
45 g (1½ oz/generous ⅓ cup)
cornflour (cornstarch)
150 ml (5 oz/⅝ cup) whipping cream

This light and stunningly pretty cake is traditionally served on Women's Day in Italy. The top of the cake is made to look like mimosa blossom by covering it in crumbled sponge. Try to find corn-fed chicken's eggs to make the sponge as it will make it all the more yellow and impressive.

Using two 20 cm (8 inch) round cake tins, start by making the sponge following the Pan di Spagna recipe on page 209.

To make the syrup, heat the water with the sugar and liqueur in a saucepan until the sugar has dissolved. Remove from the heat and allow to cool.

To make the custard, heat the milk with the vanilla in a medium saucepan until warm. In a bowl, whisk together the egg yolks, lemon zest, sugar and cornflour. Whisk in a little of the warmed milk and then pour this mixture into the saucepan with the rest of the milk. Stir with a wooden spoon until the mixture thickens, then remove from the heat. Transfer to a bowl and cover the surface with clingfilm to avoid a skin forming. Allow to cool. In a separate bowl, whip the cream to soft peaks then whisk it into the cold custard.

Meanwhile, trim the brown crusts off all sides of one of the sponge cakes and then crumble the yellow centre into a bowl using your fingers, or whizz briefly in a food processor. Cut the other sponge in half horizontally and drizzle the syrup over both sides of the cut sponge to moisten it. Put the cake on a cake board if you have one to make it easier to pick up and turn around.

Use a palette knife to spread one-third of the cream over the bottom half of the cake and carefully place the other half on top. Smother the top and sides of the cake in the remaining cream and scatter over the sponge crumbs. Transfer to a serving dish and admire your work!

TORTA CAPRESE

CHOCOLATE & ALMOND CAKE

**Serves 6–8 (makes one
22 cm/8¾ inch round cake)**

200 g (7oz/1⅓ cups) whole skinned
  almonds
200 g (7 oz) dark chocolate,
  minimum 70% cocoa solids,
  broken into squares
200 g (7 oz/¾ cup) salted butter,
  plus extra for greasing
4 eggs, separated
200 g (7 oz/⅞ cup) caster (superfine)
  sugar
icing (confectioner's) sugar, for dusting

*Little nuggets of almonds pack out this dense cake full of
wicked chocolate indulgence, which originates from Capri.
Whole peeled almonds save a lot of time and effort but if
you can only find them with skins, blanch them in boiling
water for a few minutes then rub between two tea towels –
the skins will come off quite easily.*

Grease a 22 cm (8¾ inch) loose-bottomed round tin with
butter. Preheat the oven to 180°C (350°F/Gas 4). Scatter the
almonds on a baking tray and bake for 10 minutes, or until
lightly browned. Finely chop the nuts using a large knife or
whizz in a food processor until they are the consistency of
demerara sugar.

Melt the chocolate and butter in a heatproof bowl over a
pan of barely simmering water or in a microwave, taking
care not to burn the chocolate. Remove from the heat and
allow to cool a little. In a separate bowl, whisk the egg yolks
and sugar together until light and fluffy. In another bowl,
whisk the egg whites until they form soft peaks.

Add the melted chocolate and butter to the egg yolks
and combine thoroughly. Mix in the ground almonds. Fold in
the egg whites using a whisk, metal spoon or spatula until
well combined, then pour into the prepared cake tin. Bake
in the oven for 35–40 minutes. The cake is cooked when it
forms a crust on the outside (don't expect a skewer inserted
into the cake to come out clean because the centre always
remains moist). To decorate the cake, place a doily on top
and sift over a fine layer of icing sugar, then carefully remove
the doily. Serve at room temperature with orange ice cream
(see page 227).

TORTINE
DI MANDORLE
LITTLE ALMOND CAKES

Makes 12 cakes

200 g (7 oz/1⅓ cups) skinned almonds
4 egg whites
    (approx 120 ml/4 fl oz/½ cup)
175 g (6 oz/1⅓ cups) icing
    (confectioner's) sugar
zest of 1 lemon
a few drops of almond essence
icing (confectioner's) sugar,
    for dusting

Tiny versions of these cakes are sold in the patisserie shops of Amalfi. They are just the right size to enjoy with coffee or after dinner without feeling too much guilt. I love the slight crunch of almond. These cakes contain no flour, so are suitable for those on a gluten-free diet.

Heat the oven to 180°C (350°F/Gas 4). Scatter the almonds on a baking tray and bake for 10 minutes, or until golden brown. Remove from the oven and allow to cool. Using a food processor or sharp knife, grind the almonds until they are the consistency of coarse sand.

In a bowl, whisk the egg whites together until stiff, then gently fold in the ground almonds, icing sugar, lemon zest and almond essence. Line a muffin tin (50 mm × 28 mm) with paper cases and spoon the mixture into the cases. Bake for 30 minutes, or until golden brown: a metal skewer inserted into the cakes should come out clean. Dust with icing sugar and serve.

PASTICCIOTTI

CUSTARD & CHERRY CAKES

Makes 8 cakes

For the pastry

175 g (6 oz/1⅓ cups) '00' or plain flour,
    plus extra for dusting
100 g (3½ oz/⅜ cup) caster
    (superfine) sugar
finely grated zest of ½ lemon
seeds from a vanilla pod, or a
    1 teaspoon vanilla extract
50 g (2 oz/¼ cup) lard (optional) (if not
    using, add an extra 50 g butter)
50 g (2 oz/¼ cup) butter at room
    temperature, plus extra for greasing
1 egg
1 tablespoon milk (optional)

For the filling

230 g (8 oz) Amarena Fabbri morello
    cherries in syrup, or cherries
    soaked in alcohol or syrup
1 quantity of Delizia al limone custard,
minus the lemon zest (see page 210)

icing (confectioner's) sugar, for dusting
eight 10 × 6 × 2 cm (4 × 2½ × ¾ inch)
    oval moulds, greased

These little oval pastry pies conceal a sweet filling of custard and cherry. They are just right for breakfast with a cappuccino. The best ones we found were in G.A.S, a bar perched on the cliffs above the sea. Try to use Fabbri cherries, sold in pretty blue and white jars in Italian delis. They have a unique flavour that is completely irresistible. Alternatively, use cherries soaked in alcohol or syrup. If you can't find oval moulds use small round ones or mince pie tins instead.

Start by making the pastry. Combine all the pastry ingredients in a food processor. If you're making it by hand, use your fingers to rub the flour, sugar, lemon zest, vanilla and fats together in a large bowl to a breadcrumb consistency. Keep your hands above the bowl, letting the breadcrumbs fall from a height to aerate them. Still using your hands, mix in the egg to form a firm dough. If the dough is a little dry, mix in a tablespoon of milk. This may happen if the egg is small or the flour very absorbent. Chill the pastry in the fridge for 20 minutes, wrapped in clingfilm.

To make the filling, drain the syrup from the cherries and reserve it for later. Cut the cherries in half. Roll out half the pastry to about 2 mm thick on a well-floured work surface. Cut around the moulds, leaving a 5 cm (2 inch) border all around. Press the pastry gently into the moulds, making sure it is well pressed into the sides. Refrigerate for 10 minutes, then trim the edges with a sharp knife.

Half-fill the moulds with the custard and place 3 cherries on top. Pipe or spoon in more custard so that the moulds are three-quarters full. Roll out the remaining pastry to about 1 mm thick again and cover the moulds with a pastry lid. Trim the edges. Prick 2 holes in the pastry with the tip of a sharp knife and refrigerate for 10 minutes.

Preheat the oven to 180°C (350°F/Gas 4). Place the moulds on a baking tray and bake for 20–25 minutes. Remove from the oven and leave to cool on a wire rack for about 30 minutes before turning out and dusting with icing sugar. Serve warm or at room temperature.

SORBETTO O GRANITA AL LIMONE

LIMONCELLO SORBET OR GRANITA

Serves 4–6

200 g (7 oz/⅞ cup) caster (superfine) sugar
400 ml (13 fl oz/1¾ cups) water
100 ml (3½ fl oz/½ cup) limoncello
juice of 5 lemons
pinch of salt

In many of the restaurants along the coast you will see lemon sorbet served in a hollowed-out lemon shell. But lemons aren't the only fruit they use in this way – you can see strawberry sorbet served in large strawberries, walnut ice cream scooped into walnut shells, etc. A selection of these makes a stunning dessert. This recipe also works for granita – the frozen ice that is scraped into little ice crystals with a spoon. There is a bar in Positano where they make the refreshing L'Albertissimo, named after the owner, which is lemon granita mixed with peach vodka and grenadine.

TO MAKE SORBET

In a small pan, heat the water with the sugar. As soon as the sugar dissolves remove the pan from the heat and pour the liquid into a refrigerated bowl to cool. Stir in the remaining ingredients, then churn in an ice-cream maker. If you don't have an ice-cream maker, make a granita instead.

TO MAKE GRANITA

In a small pan, heat the water with the sugar. As soon as the sugar dissolves remove the pan from the heat and pour the liquid into a refrigerated bowl to cool. Stir in the remaining ingredients, then pour the cooled mixture into a shallow container and freeze until solid. Use a spoon to break the mixture into large crystals and refreeze.

TRAMONTO IN AMALFI

SUNSET IN AMALFI

Serves 4–6

For the orange ice cream
zest and juice of 2 oranges
350 ml (12 fl oz/1½ cups) milk
350 ml (12 fl oz/1½ cups) double cream
6 egg yolks
225 g (8 oz/1 cup) caster (superfine)
   sugar

For the lemon ice cream
zest and juice of 3 lemons
350 ml (12 fl oz/1½ cups) milk
350 ml (12 fl oz/1½ cups) double cream
6 egg yolks
225 g (8 oz/1 cup) caster (superfine)
   sugar

Strawberry sauce (see page 230),
   to serve

I loved the combination, and yes, the sugar-sweet name of this ice cream that I saw in a shop in Amalfi. Lemon and orange ice creams were swirled together and served with a strawberry sauce. Spectacular to look at and even better to eat! There is something splendid about rich custard ice cream made with citrus fruits.

To make the orange ice cream, peel the zest of 1 orange into long lengths using a potato peeler, omitting as much of the white pith as possible. Heat the milk and cream along with the orange zest in a pan over a medium heat to just below boiling point (if using a thermometer it should read between 75°C/167°F and 80°C/176°F). Meanwhile, beat the egg yolks and sugar together in a bowl until smooth.

When the milk and cream have reached the right heat, add a ladleful of the liquid to the beaten eggs, stirring constantly. Pour this mixture back into the milk pan and whisk on a low heat, bringing the custard up to just below boiling point (85°C/185°F). The mixture will thicken and should coat the back of a wooden spoon. Do not allow it to boil or it will separate. Remove the pan from the heat and mix in the juice of both oranges. Strain through a sieve into a bowl and stir in the finely grated zest of the remaining orange. Set this bowl over a larger bowl filled with iced water to cool the mixture quickly. As soon as it is cold, churn in an ice-cream maker.

To make the lemon ice cream, follow the method for making the orange ice cream.

To make the Sunset in Amalfi, spoon the orange and lemon ice creams into a container, together with a few tablespoons of the strawberry sauce swirled through – you will soon see the streaks of sunset appearing. Don't worry if it looks messy at this stage. Freeze overnight and serve with a little extra strawberry sauce.

GELATO DI YOGURT AI FRUTTI DI BOSCO
YOGHURT ICE CREAM WITH BERRY COULIS

Serves 6–8

250 ml (8½ fl oz/1 cup) milk
250 g (9 oz/1⅛ cups) caster
    (superfine) sugar
750 g (1 lb 10 oz/3 cups) Greek yoghurt
fresh berries, to serve

Heat the milk and sugar in a saucepan over a medium heat until the sugar has dissolved and you can't feel any crystals on the bottom of the pan. Tip the yoghurt into a cold metal bowl and pour the milk over. Set the bowl over a larger bowl filled with iced water to cool the mixture quickly. When cold, churn in an ice-cream maker. Serve scattered with fresh berries.

SORBETTO DI LAMPONI
RASPBERRY SORBET

500 g (1 lb 2 oz/4 cups) raspberries
75 ml (2½ fl oz/¼ cup) water
20 g (¾ oz) powdered glucose
100 g (3½ oz/⅜ cup) caster
    (superfine) sugar

This recipe contains powdered glucose, which helps to aerate the sorbet and keep it soft in the freezer. This is how a lot of commercial ice creams and sorbets are made. Powdered glucose is available from chemists, Asian stores and online.

Blend the raspberries in a food processor or with a hand-held blender and then pass through a fine sieve. Transfer the coulis to a saucepan with the water. In a bowl, mix the powdered glucose with the sugar and tip into the pan. Warm over a medium heat to dissolve the sugar. Transfer to a bowl. Set the bowl over a larger bowl filled with iced water to cool the mixture quickly. When cold, churn in an ice-cream maker.

VARIATION
Use strawberries or woodland fruits instead of the raspberries.

SALSA DI FRAGOLE
STRAWBERRY SAUCE

Serves 6-8

500 g (1 lb 2 oz/3⅓ cups) strawberries
50–100 g (2–3½ oz/¼–⅜ cup) caster
(superfine) sugar

Try making this with strawberries, raspberries or a combination of both. It is the most versatile sauce to have in the fridge, adding a burst of flavour to a bowl of thick yoghurt with sliced banana or vanilla ice cream, and also looks fantastic swirled into a glass of Prosecco.

Hull the strawberries and cut any large ones in half. Tip into a large saucepan and add the sugar, according to the sweetness of the fruit. Bring to a gentle boil and cook for 15–20 minutes, or until the strawberries give easily when squished against the side of the pan. Strain through a sieve into a jug and when cool store covered in the fridge, for up to 1 week.

TIRAMISÙ FRAGOLE & LIMONE
QUICK STRAWBERRY & LEMON TIRAMISU

Serves 6

500 g (1 lb 2oz/3⅓ cups) strawberries
300 ml (10 fl oz/1¼ cups) whipping
cream
250 g (9 oz) mascarpone
zest and juice of 2 lemons
100 g (3½ oz/⅜ cup) caster
(superfine) sugar
2 tablespoons maraschino liqueur,
white wine or elderflower cordial
½–1 quantity of Strawberry sauce
(see above)
12 sponge fingers
icing (confectioner's) sugar, for dusting

This is a great quick dessert to make. Served in individual glasses it is very impressive to look at. We first tried it in Positano in a lovely restaurant called Next 2.

Set aside six medium strawberries. In a bowl, whip the cream and then whisk in the mascarpone. Fold in the lemon zest and sugar, followed by the lemon juice. In a flat dish, mix the liqueur with 1½ tablespoons of the strawberry sauce, then dip the sponge fingers into the liqueur until they are just soft but not soggy. Cut the remaining strawberries into slices. Lay a few slices in the bottom of 6 Martini glasses or tumblers so that the slices are facing outwards, then add a layer of cream, the remaining sauce and the soaked sponge fingers. Finish with a layer of cream. Decorate each glass with a fanned strawberry and lightly dust with icing sugar.

MARMELLATA DI LIMONE

LEMON MARMALADE

Makes about 6 × 340 g (12 oz) jars

1 kg (2 lb 3 oz) unwaxed organic lemons
200–500 ml (7–17 fl oz/⅞–2⅛ cups)
    apple juice
about 1.5 kg (3 lb 5 oz) caster
    (superfine) sugar

Lemon marmalade is often used to refresh the palette after eating anchovies. I love it stirred into Greek yoghurt for breakfast.

Scrub the lemons and put them into a large heavy-based preserving pan. Pour the water over and cover the surface with a circle of baking parchment to trap in the steam. Bring to the boil and simmer for about 2 hours, or until the skins are tender. This can be done the night before and allowed to cool overnight.

Preheat the oven to 110°C (225°F/Gas ¼). Using tongs remove the lemons from the pan and put into a colander over a bowl. Pour the cooking liquor into a measuring jug and set aside.

Cut the lemons into 5 mm (¼ inch) cubes and put into a large bowl. Discard the pips but pour any juice into the measuring jug, with the rest of the cooking liquor. Top up to 1 litre with the apple juice. Weigh the cubes of lemon flesh; they should weigh between 600 and 800 g (1 lb 5 oz and 1 lb 12 oz). Now weigh out twice the amount of sugar.

Put spotlessly clean glass jars upside down on a rack in the oven for at least 20 minutes to sterilize them, then remove from the oven.

Put the cut fruit and liquid into the preserving pan and pour in the sugar. Bring to the boil for 30–60 minutes, until the jam reaches setting point. Test the setting point by dropping a teaspoon of jam on a freezing cold saucer: after about a minute the jam should trickle slowly down the plate when tipped and wrinkle when you push a finger through it. This will give you a soft set ideal for pouring over yoghurt or ice cream. For a thicker spreading consistency more like marmalade, leave it to boil for a little longer. This time, when poured

onto a freezing cold saucer it will look more like a jelly after 2 minutes. When testing, remember to remove the pan from the heat so that you don't over-boil the jam.

When you are happy with the set, remove the pan from the heat and skim any scum from the surface. Allow to rest for 10 minutes to help distribute the fruit evenly through the jam. Fill the sterilized jars, seal and leave to cool. The jam will keep for up to 6 months in a dark cool cupboard.

MARMELLATA DI PERE
PEAR JAM

This pretty pink jam is very popular in Amalfi. It is spread on pecorino cheese and served either for breakfast or as an appetizer with bread. It is made from pere pennate. The fruit doesn't mature on the trees and is picked before it is ripe and stored on sloping roofs facing the sun until the day it is eaten as a fruit or made into this delicious jam. If the pears are very hard you will have to boil them for longer.

Makes about 5 × 340 g (12 oz) jars

1.5 kg (3 lb 5 oz) pears
1 litre (34 fl oz/4¼ cups) water
juice of 2 lemons
1 kg (2 lb 3 oz) caster (superfine) sugar

Peel and dice the pears into 2 cm (¾ inch) cubes. As you cut them, put them into a large heavy-based preserving pan, along with the water and lemon juice. Boil for 15–30 minutes, or until just tender. Add the sugar and boil vigorously for a further 30–60 minutes, or until the liquid has the consistency of syrup when dropped onto a freezing cold plate (see Lemon marmalade, opposite, for setting points). Allow the jam to cool for 10 minutes and then use a hand-held blender or liquidizer to partially purée the jam to your liking. I like a bit of texture in my jam, so I don't blend it too much. Boil the jam again for just a few minutes. Sterilize the jars (see opposite) and bottle as with the Lemon marmalade.

COCKTAIL
& BIBITE

COCKTAILS
& DRINKS

Since the sunsets in Amalfi are so spectacular a big deal is made of terraces that can boast a view, and of course a range of delicious drinks is offered to enhance the experience. However, many of the drinks available have sober roots: liqueurs such as **limoncello** and the walnut-based **nocillo** were originally made by monks and administered as medicinal or digestive aids (or so they said!)

Concerto is a herb- and coffee-based liqueur from Tramonti and Maiori. Its recipe is jealously guarded by the monks and families who still make it from a formula devised many centuries ago by the inhabitants of the San Francesco di Tramonti monastery. **Finocchietto** is a pale aniseed-flavoured liqueur made from the seeds of the wild fennel that grows in abundance on the hills. It too is often taken as a digestive. Rare but delicious is **fragolino**, made from tiny wild strawberries.

While we watched the last rays of the sun set over Positano, we enjoyed aperitifs on the stunning terrace at San Pietro.

ROSMARINO

ROSEMARY & LIME GIN FIZZ

For the rosemary and lime syrup
(makes 30 cocktails)
4 long sprigs of rosemary
450 g (1lb/2 cups) caster (superfine)
    sugar
2 limes, juiced and zest peeled into
    lengths
500 ml (17 fl oz/generous 2 cups) water

For the cocktail
gin
ice
soda or tonic water
wedge of lime for each glass
sprig of rosemary for each glass

While we watched the last rays of the sun set over Positano, we enjoyed aperitifs on the stunning terrace at San Pietro. Sprigs of rosemary from the herb gardens perfumed this refreshing and unusual drink. I liked it so much I had to recreate my own version back home.

To make the syrup, put all the ingredients in a saucepan and bring to the boil, then lower the heat and simmer for 10 minutes. Remove from the heat and leave to cool. Line a sieve with muslin or a thin cloth and pour over a kettle-full of boiling water to sterilize it. Strain the syrup through the cloth into a sterilized jug and then into sterilized bottles and store in the fridge for up to 3 weeks.

   To make the cocktail, pour 30 ml (1 fl oz/2 tablespoons) syrup and 50 ml (2 fl oz/¼ cup) gin over ice, top with soda or tonic water and serve with a wedge of lime and a rosemary sprig.

LIMONCELLO
LEMON LIQUEUR

8 medium organic unwaxed lemons
1.5 litres (2½ pints/6 cups) 95% pure
    alcohol, or good-quality
    unflavoured vodka
2 litres (3½ pints/8½ cups) water
1 kg (2 lb 3 oz/8 cups) caster
    (superfine) sugar

The simple blend of lemons, sugar and alcohol makes this one of the easiest liqueurs to make. It needs no additives or preservatives to keep but is best stored in the freezer as it should be served really cold. Pure alcohol is hard to get hold of in most countries, and so vodka is the next best option. You can also find **crema di limone***, which is limoncello with added cream, or even* **cioccolata al limoncello***, which has the addition of cocoa powder.* **Mandarino, arancino** *and* **meloncello** *are made using a similar process with mandarins, oranges and melons. All are worth a try, though to my mind nothing beats a freezing cold shot of limoncello to bring you to your senses – or maybe that should be away from your senses!*

Cut the ends off the lemons. Using a vegetable peeler, peel the lemon zest as thinly as possible, trying not to remove any of the bitter white pith. Put the zest and alcohol in a large clean glass jar and leave to steep for 10–14 days.

After that time, pour the water into a large saucepan, add the sugar and dissolve over a medium heat. Remove from the heat and allow to cool, then add to the lemons and the alcohol. Mix well and strain through a fine sieve, then decant into bottles and store in the freezer. Do not fill the bottles right to the top to allow for expansion should the liqueur freeze. The high alcohol content should prevent this happening but some vodkas just might. Drink straight from the freezer in shot glasses after a meal.

WAYS TO USE LIMONCELLO
To enjoy your homemade limoncello as part of a cocktail, pour a shot into a flute and top with Prosecco. For a prettier version, make a Sunset: pour a shot of limoncello into a highball glass and top with orange juice followed by a shot of grenadine, which will sink to the bottom of the glass.

Watching the warm sun set over Positano from the most glamourous hotel terrace on the coastline, sparkling glass of Bellini in one hand, husband holding the other — well, it was pretty damn perfect.

BELLINI
PROSECCO WITH WHITE PEACH NECTAR

Serves 6

250 g (9 oz) white peach (approx 2–3 peaches) flesh, peeled and stones removed

25 g (1 oz/2 tablespoons) caster (superfine) sugar

1 bottle Prosecco

Try to get hold of ripe white peaches to make the purée for their amazing floral scent. If you can't find them, use yellow peaches instead. If you're struggling to find ripe peaches, soften them by heating them with the sugar until tender.

Cut the peach flesh into 3 cm (1 inch) cubes and tip into a bowl. Mix in the sugar and leave to macerate for 30–60 minutes. Blend the fruit to a soft purée; it should pour easily. If the mixture is too thick, add a little water to dilute it.

To make the Bellini, pour all the purée into a jug along with a glass of Prosecco and stir – it will fizz and foam. Pour into glasses and top with Prosecco straight from the bottle.

VARIATION
For a strawberry version of this drink, called Rossini, replace the peach purée with the strawberry sauce on page 230.

MARTINI PEPERONCINO
CHILLI MARTINI

Mix two parts of Martini Extra Dry and one part of chilli vodka, pour into a Martini glass and garnish with an olive. To make the chilli vodka, simply immerse a long red chilli in a bottle of vodka and leave for at least 2 weeks. The strength will intensify with time, so beware! Chilli vodka makes a mean Bloody Mary too.

CAFFÉ

Coffee drinking starts young, as young as seven or eight years old, diluted with milk. As with any medicine or pick-me-up, vital shots of caffeine are taken at precise intervals, dispensed to the 'patients' from the multitude of bars, along with a dose of gossip, laughter or lamentation. Naples is said to be the heart of espresso and each Neapolitan – and for that matter Amalfitano – will have their own strong opinions on where to get their life-giving shot of the dark elixir.

Caffè, in the form of a cappuccino or caffè latte, is taken lukewarm at the bar with a croissant or doughnut to celebrate the morning. As Italians don't like to drink milk after a main meal, cappuccino is not taken again after breakfast. The Italian equivalent of elevenses consists of a quick espresso or caffè macchiato (a coffee with 2–3 teaspoons of hot or cold milk) at the bar, or a caffè lungo (a coffee longer than an espresso but not as long as a caffè Americano). The same would be taken after lunch to help with digestion. The final coffee of the day is drunk at a bar after dinner, while enjoying a passeggiata, a gentle walk through the town often wearing one's finest clothes.

In hot weather, caffè shakerato or caffè freddo are versions of iced coffee. Espresso with a shred of lemon zest makes a refreshing twist on a regular coffee, and some Italians say this is a good cure for a headache. Typical of Naples are Caffè Kimbo, Caffè Kosé and Lavazza. Kimbo was a brand started by Café do Brasil in the 1950s and became a national success story.

The best coffee on the Amalfi Coast is said to be served at the G.A.S bar, which stands for Guglielmo, Antonella and Salvatore. I spoke with Guglielmo who said good coffee is down to the type and roasting of the beans, along with looking after the coffee machine and ensuring the pressure is just right. He told me that without love there is no point.

Good grief, I thought, how many baristi outside Italy feel such passion? The coffee was indeed perfect; I sipped a cappuccino whose temperature neither scalded nor chilled my lips. Everything was in the right proportions: one-third coffee, one-third milk and one-third froth. Gugliemo is so passionate about coffee, and in our opinion the G.A.S bar does indeed deserve its local reputation for the best coffee on the Amalfi Coast.

FORMAGGI
___
CHEESE

*Cheese is often eaten with honey or jams in Italy, a habit I have taken to at home. We visited Antonietta and Antonio Neclerio's dairy farm in Agerola, in the central area of the Amalfi Peninsula. They have been making cheese for over thirty years. Their cows are in a stable at the back of the dairy and are milked twice a day. They produce ricotta, **fior di latte**, butter and **caciocavallo** every day. Here are some of the typical cheeses of the Sorrentine Peninsula.*

CACIOCAVALLO

This southern Italian speciality is traditionally made from the curds of the milk of *podolica* cows. There are two types of caciocavalli: *morbido*, which is soft, and the hard, longer-matured *stagionato*, which can be grated over pasta instead of Parmesan or Grana Padano. The name translates as 'cheese on horseback', perhaps because pairs of this cheese are bound together with rope and left to hang a *cavallo*, either side of a stick, to mature.

FIOR DI LATTE

A cow's milk cheese with a similar texture to mozzarella, it is often used as a topping on pizza in preference to buffalo milk cheese as it is less watery.

MOZZARELLA DI BUFALA

Mozzarella is the generic name for soft cheeses made by spinning and pinching off balls of curd, and is traditionally eaten very fresh – within a day or so of being made. Classic (PDO) *mozzarella di bufala* is made solely from the milk of water buffalo, which have been found ideally suited to the marshy grasslands of the Campania region since late Roman times, though it's increasingly now made from a mixture of cow and buffalo milk. In the Amalfi region, buffalo mozzarella is produced in Tramonti, a group of hamlets in the rising land of the Latteri hills at the foot of the Sorrentine Peninsula.

On the walls of the old cowshed caper plants with full, ripe berries tumbled down. Rosemary plants grew between the cracks in the stones.

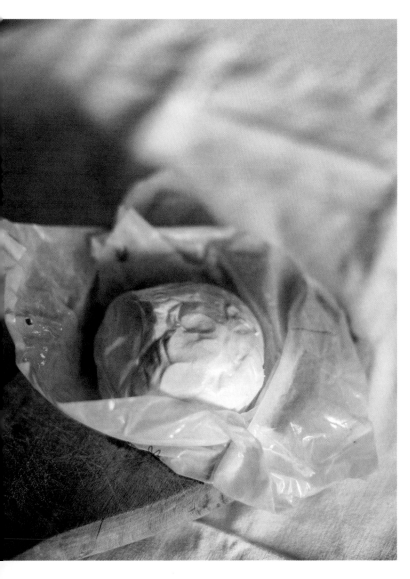

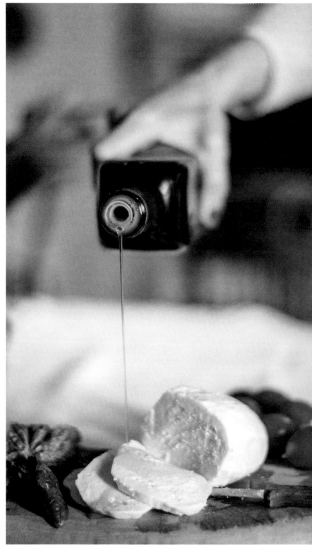

PECORINO

A ewe's milk cheese made all over central and southern Italy, this is produced in two forms, *pecorino stagionato* is made from reheated curd and matured to form a hard cheese that can be grated over pasta or eaten with honey. *Pecorino fresco* is much softer and less mature. It is good for cooking or eating on its own.

PROVOLA

This is a pulled curd cheese made from the milk of either cows or buffalo, or from a mixture of the two. In Campania there is a smoked variety called *provola affumicata*.

PROVOLONE DEL MONACO

Provolone is a hard, mature cheese with a strong flavour, often used instead of Parmesan in cooking or eaten alone or with jam. It is made in the Latteri mountains from the milk of *razza agerolese* cows.

SCAMORZA

A pulled cheese made from cow's milk, although sometimes also with buffalo milk, this is formed into a pear shape, often with a string tied round the narrow end. It is eaten fresh or *affumicata*, (smoked), and may be grilled.

RICOTTA

This famous cheese is made from runny whey with a little more milk and salt added. It is then cooked slowly until it reaches 90°C (194°F): 'Slowly, slowly' I was told by Antonietta Neclerio, 'until it flowers at the top.' The heating process makes the liquid split into soft white lumps that rise to the surface above the clear watery whey. Antonietta takes a long-handled slotted spoon and skims the surface to collect the curds. She lowers them gently into white plastic forms to drain further. These are then cooled and sold the same day. The consistency and flavour are a world away from the mass-produced ricotta we see in our supermarkets. The Agerolese ricotta is used to make desserts such as *pastiera napoletana* and *sfogliatelle*, or it can be eaten drizzled with a little local honey.

What an amazing year we have had working with these two wonderful women, Helen Cathcart, Photographer, and Kate Pollard, Commissioning Editor. Helen's photos make our food sing and Kate's ability to channel our enthusiasm onto the page was indispensible. Both pour experience, knowledge and love into their work and yet manage to be fun too. Designer Clare Skeats has done a great job on this beautiful book, thank you. And to the ever-smiling Manjula, for all her hard work and washing up!

We would like to say a big thank you to the following people, their generosity with their time and wonderful food was inspiring:

Enza and Rino Milano
Ristorante Il Pirata
Via Terramare
84010 Praiano (SA) Italia
www.ristoranteilpirata.net

Giovanni Di Bianco
Il Giardiniello
17, Corso Vittorio Emanuele
84010 Minori (SA) Italia
www.ristorantegiardiniello.com

Francesco Tammaro
Ristorante San Pietro
Piazzetta S. Francesco, 2
Cetara SA Italia
www.sanpietroristorante.it

Gianfranco Cioffi from
Zero Ristorante Pizzeria
12 High Street
Ware, sg12 9bx
Herts UK
www.zero-ristorante.co.uk

Netta Bottone
Cumpa' Cosimo
Via Roma 44–46
Ravello (SA) Italia
Tel: 0039 089 857156

Andrea Pansa Pasticceria
Piazza Duomo 40
84011 Amalfi, Italia
www.pasticceriapansa.it

Sal de Riso Pasticceria
Minori (SA) Italia
www.salderiso.it

Next 2 Ristorante
Via Pasitea 242
84017 Positano (SA) Italia
www.next2.it

Clelia Del Gaizo
Bar Mare
Via Marina di Praia 9
Praiano (SA)

Nicola Giannullo
Ristorante Rabbit
Via S.Lorenzo 98
80051 Agerola (NA)
www.rabbitagerola.it

Faith Manna and Michelina
Villa Michelina
Praiano (SA) Italia
www.amalfivacations.com

Villa Cimbrone
Via S Chiara 26
84010 Ravello (SA) Italia
www.villacimbrone.com

Trattoria da Gemma
Via fra Gerardo Sasso 11
84011 Amalfi (SA)
www.trattoriadagemma.com

Antonietta and Antonio Neclerio
(Dairy)
Agerola (NA)
Italia

First row left to right:
Enza Milano, Michelina,
Gregorio Piazza

Second row left to right:
Giovanni Di Bianco,
Helen Cathcart, Stefano Borella

Third row left to right:
Vincenzo Di Monda,
Gianfranco Cioffi,
Francesco Tammaro

INDEX

NB: page numbers in *italic* indicate colour plates

Indexer's note: garlic, olive oil and onion are used in most recipes and none are therefore indexed

ABOUT THE AUTHORS

Owners of London's Caffé Caldesi, Caldesi in Campagna in Bray, and the Marylebone La Cucina Caldesi cooking school, Katie and Giancarlo Caldesi have a passion for Italian food. They have spent over 10 years teaching students at every level, and have written several cookbooks. Katie and Giancarlo have two children, Giorgio and Flavio.

Wild Rosemary & Lemon Cake by Katie and Giancarlo Caldesi

First published in 2013 by Hardie Grant Books
Hardie Grant Books (UK)
Dudley House, North Suit 34–35 Southampton Street
London WC2E 7HF
www.hardiegrant.co.uk

Hardie Grant Books (Australia)
Ground Floor, Building 1
658 Church Street
Melbourne, VIC 3121
www.hardiegrant.com.au

British Library Cataloguing-in-Publication Data. A catalogue record for this book is available from the British Library.

ISBN 978-1-74270-632-0

Commissioning Editor: Kate Pollard
Cover and Internal design: Clare Skeats
Photography and retouching: Helen Cathcart
Endpaper illustration: Tom Clohosy Cole
Colour reproduction by p2D

Printed and bound China by 1010 Printing International Limited

10 9 8 7 6 5 4 3 2 1

Agerola

Positano

Furore

Praiano

Conca dei Marini

LA COSTIERA AMALFITANA